Joy is a Jewel

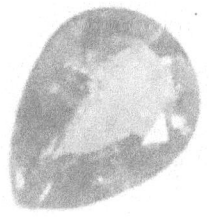

Rev. Carolyn Anne Venable

Copyright © 2016 by Carolyn Anne Venable

All rights reserved solely by the author. The author guarantees all contents are original and do not infringe upon the legal rights of any other person or work. No part of this publication may be reproduced, stored in a retrieval system, or transmitted in any form by any means—electronic, mechanical, digital photocopy, recording, or any other without the prior permission of the author.

Most Scriptures are from the English Standard Version unless noted.

7710-T Cherry Park Dr, Ste 224
Houston, TX 77095
http://WorldwidePublishingGroup.com

Printed in the United States of America

eBook: 978-3-9602-8073-6
Paperback: 978-0692710197
Hardcover: 978-1-60796-541-1

Table of Contents

DEDICATION 5

PREFACE 7

INTRODUCTION 9

PURE JOY 13

JOY AND HAPPINESS 21

THE #1 JOY SAPPER 49

A WORLD FULL OF JOY 55

THANKFULNESS 93

THE JOYS OF THE KINGDOM 103

THE SONG OF JOY 131

THE BEATITUDES 155

THE JOY OF OTHERS 193

THE JOY OF LOVE 203

THE JOY OF JOYS 215

DEDICATION

FOR THE BRIDE OF CHRIST

Psalm 45:13-15

"All glorious is the princess in her chamber,

with robes interwoven with gold.

In many-colored robes, she is led to the King,

with her virgin companions following behind her.

With JOY and GLADNESS, they are led along

as they enter the palace of the King."

PREFACE

Face it. I'm not always joyful. This past year (2015) has been one of my hardest. I had put away writing this book. The enemy of my soul likes to come and try to steal my joy because joy is one of my stronger gifts. Yet, anyone whose joy had been taken from them could never be qualified to write on this subject!

While preparing a draft, the enemy hit me with a wallop, in the way of a stroke. I also had a fractured arm, about six months later. And all this time, I'm working on this book, a book on joy! It was as if the devils of hell had conspired against me. They wanted to defeat me.

A few months after my stroke, a man of God called to encourage me: I was *supposed* to write this book. I began to cry. "How can I write a book on joy?" He spoke, and as he spoke, the laughter just welled up inside of me. There was **JOY!**

I then asked the LORD to return to me seven-fold of what the enemy had stolen from me. He had stolen some of my **JOY!**

"But if he is caught, he will pay sevenfold; he will give all the goods of his house." Proverbs 6:31

What the enemy had stolen wasn't my sole source of joy. My source of joy is greater. It's an unending source, and it's always available. It is Christ Himself.

O JOY OF JOYS

O Joy of Joys! Your mercies new each morning
Make me to rise up from the cold, dark night
O warm my soul and fill my heart with longing
For You alone upon Your throne of light.

O Joy of Joys! Such lilting joy and wonder
To see Your majesty now fill this place.
O Joy of Joys! The beauty and the splendor!
O Joy of Joys! To know Your glory, truth and grace!

O You shall come at trumpet's sound some morning.
Darkness retreats and all fall at Your feet.
O Joy of Joys! To now behold My Lord and King!
O Joy of Joys! And rhapsody so sweet!

© Copyright 2000 HIM/CAVenable

May be sung to the traditional "Londonderry Air" melody ("Danny Boy")

INTRODUCTION

"WHO IS SUFFICIENT FOR THESE THINGS?"

Sad. So Sad. "No one was happy except me," a brother in the LORD informed me. In an office/factory of sixty-two people, that is pretty sad. A booming business and more money didn't satisfy it. The associates were still aggravated! They were always fussing about something, especially their spouses.

Happiness can be elusive. But there is great joy to be found in the Kingdom of God!

"The joy of the Lord is my strength!" Truly, truly! "The joy of the Lord is my strength!" Nehemiah 8:10

"Your joy is contagious!" "Your joy is anointed!" These are some of the compliments said of me. Folks could recognize my laugh across a crowded room. One pastor told me I was the happiest person he knew!

I did a camp for the children of Chernobyl. The Belorussian counselor told me that the most important value that I had instilled amongst the children was to have "modeled joy" for them. Some cultures are not quite so happy. Sad. So I continued in ministry to children, spreading joy and happiness over many years.

Yet I have had sad times. I fought against depression and despair. Perhaps it has been those very battles that the LORD used to strengthen me.

My life, like yours and everyone else's, has not always been a serenade. My mother died when I was eight, resulting in a dysfunctional family. As a young mother, I literally went through a flood and a fire in one month's time! I had twenty years of praying for an unsaved husband who was opposed to my even being a Christian. Some of these stories are shared in this book, lest you think I'm joyful because I haven't known sorrow. It is quite the opposite!

But I've learned to overcome! The **JOY** just keeps popping up as the Holy Spirit renews my strength!

I write these words as I struggle through illness. "Who is sufficient for these things?" My Father encourages me. I listen to His comforts and directions. My flesh is weak, right now, very weak. I acknowledge it. I know that I am not always chipper, but who then is? Nevertheless, I have **JOY** that no man, no devil can take away! Even though my body is wilting, my roots in Christ run deep.

There is a little smile in my heart. I don't feel well enough to jump around happily and smile and laugh, but I have a smile in my heart. I know He loves me and that is my wellspring of joy, gurgling underneath the surface of my weakened flesh. I can feel it on the inside, even though it isn't surfacing right now. Soon it will breakthrough. I have joy deep within and it will bubble up. I am full of joy in my inner man. My outer man languishes. My inner man jumps for joy!

Through trials and tribulations, the LORD Himself is my joy! Despite and through my circumstances, and by the grace of God, I have **joy unspeakable**! And you can have it, too, because joy is a gift from God to you!

The perspective of this book is not psychological, although it includes some practical help for happiness. This book is based on the eternal truth of Scripture. "Faith comes by hearing and hearing by the word of God..." (Romans 10:17) So take these many joyous Scriptures to heart and be encouraged!

May this book, filled with spiritual nuggets of joy, be a blessing to you. **Joy** to you, dear one! May you be filled to overflowing and bubble over with contagious **JOY**! Then share your **JOY** with others!

PURE JOY

"I HAVE LOVED YOU"

I was sick and getting sicker. On May 22, 2015, it culminated in a stroke. Thankfully, my husband was home. It could've been that he was at the office that day, but I had wanted to go to the emergency room due to my illness. I stepped out of the shower, and then it hit. I suffered the stroke.

Being at the hospital seven days, there was plenty of opportunity to do a thoughtful reflection. I really wondered what was going on with me spiritually. I wanted to hear from the LORD. I wondered why I didn't hear from the LORD. Day after day in the hospital, I lay and I didn't hear His voice to me.

But His Holy Spirit in me, rose up and I prayed forcefully in the Spirit. Now, that was something! The Holy Spirit prayed through me! It was an awesome moment, awesome in that I could barely speak. When you have a stroke, you just don't talk. My natural language, though I could think straight, was not coming out. Yet, I could pray in ever-flowing tongues. This was marvelous to me.

My lack of speech did not affect, for the most part, my singing. I came home and started to play the piano and sing, a little rough at first.

But I was back in the hospital within a week. Not a stroke, but the other incident that led me into the stroke. I had a condition known as ulcerative colitis. They once again told me, because I have had this happen before ten years earlier, that I would have to have my large intestines taken out. That didn't happen, praise God!

My prognosis was to see if medicines could alleviate my condition. After six days in the hospital, I was home with a ton of prescriptions to take.

(It appears that Sorbitol [a sweetener] was the source of my gastrointestinal problems. I had chewed sugar-free gum [with Sorbitol] almost every day. Some suggest that Sorbitol is a gastrointestinal irritant because it doesn't digest properly.)

My recuperative times were days of singing to the Lord and reading portions of Scripture. Then I heard from Him. I was about to close the piano and go. But I heard the Holy Spirit saying to write a song.

"This is my song to you. And you will sing it before crowds of people. Yet I will come to you and sing it personally. This is my song to you."

I sat down and immediately wrote, "I have loved you. I have loved you with an everlasting love." Ah, sweetness! God was speaking His love for me! "With an everlasting love"! Oh, the joy of that moment!

A month later of my last hospital stay, on July 5th, 2015, I was back to lead worship at church. A little hesitant, but they prayed for me and I made it through.

It amazed the people that I led worship at our annual conference in July. If you were in a real lengthy discussion with me, I was a little less than coherent, but that was not the point. I was there. At the end of the conference, I played my song, "I Have Loved You."

God allowed this. He did it to prove that the devil is a liar. I was supposed to have started full-time as music minister in the beginning of June. I couldn't. But I was determined to play because that is my calling. I started a little late ... but with God on time! God was just going to show what He could do with me. To God be the glory!

God allowed this. God used this to show me how much my husband loved me. He really did! My husband struggled almost to the point of exhaustion through my weeks of illness, visiting me at the hospital and giving me my medication, cooking, washing clothes, and all that with a hectic attorney's profession to boot! I cried with tears of joy, the many times I thought of it afterward.

The love of Christ was extended to me in my hour of need. My husband and all my children were there. My sister and her clan came in from California. My church was there, some ministers of the Lord, and even some people I didn't see often were there.

"God allowed this," a prophet of God told me. "You have not cursed God." And I hadn't.

The attack of the enemy came. But my sweet husband really, really loving me was a far purer **joy!** That **joy** far out did the pain it took. If you wait, God always brings forth the **JOY** of victory and we all have victory in Christ!

"WE WILL SING FOR JOY OVER YOUR VICTORY."

Psalm 20:5

"I Have Loved You"

Verse
Who can separate us from the love of Christ!
Who can keep us apart?
Who can separate us from the love of Christ!
Yes, you have stolen my heart!

Chorus
I have loved you; I have loved you
With an everlasting love
I have loved you; I have loved you
With an everlasting love

Verse
The breadth, length, height and depth beyond conception
Of the love lavished on us
To know the love of Christ that exceeds perception,
His love so boundless! His love so boundless!
His love so boundless!

Chorus
I have saved you; I have saved you
With an everlasting love
I have saved you; I have saved you
With an everlasting love

Bridge
Many waters cannot quench love,
Neither floods drown it, too.
Christ gave Himself up, up for love,
A fragrant offering, a sacrifice…for you.

And I love you! (Repeat 3 times)

© Copyright 2015 HIM.CAVenable

SHEER JOY

We were dancing outdoors in the mountains of France, praising the LORD with flowing banners waving in the air to the music. That's when it hit me. A moment of sheer elation and joy. In that memorable moment, I knew that I was smack dab in the center of God's perfect will for my life! It was sheer joy!

Seventeen little girls, ages about eight to ten, from the Chernobyl-contaminated country of Belarus, were spending three weeks in the mountains of France. It was a time of restoration for the health of our little Belarusian guests. The LORD had given me a dream instructing me specifically to do this camp and here it was accomplished by His grace! Yes, God cares for the hurting. He is looking for us to be His hands to touch. If you want joy, go touch someone with the love of Christ, in the name of Christ.

This was their first camp for these girls. They were having an experience of a lifetime, both physically and spiritually. Me, too. I was fulfilling the will of God for my life, seeing a vision come to pass. Our Spirit-given theme for that camp was "The Fruit of the Spirit" and the fruit of joy was certainly evident. It was my joy to give, to share the joy of the LORD, to show these children that there is joy in the Presence of the LORD.

It was here that the Belorussian counselor told me that the most important thing that I had done for the children was to have "modeled joy" for them. It was my delight. We laughed. We sang. We danced before the LORD. We had a picnic. The children were grateful for even the smallest of treats! We gave them little French dolls as gifts. We showered them with affection and hugs. Their smiles warmed our hearts.

Oh, we had some problems, too, and some rainy weather. Some of the little girls got car sick on the winding mountain roads when we went on outings. But those were mere little bumps compared to the mountain-top joys we all shared that summer. On the twisty roads of life, we may have some upsets, but the view at the final destination is worth it - if you're headed towards the King and His Kingdom of joy and glory!

We ended our happy time together with the girls' first ice cream sundae party. Joy was overflowing, but it was sad to part. We hugged and cried and said good-bye. But we can look forward to seeing each other again with shining faces in heaven's glory! It'll be sheer **JOY!**

JOY AND HAPPINESS

THE MEANING OF JOY

Joy is "the emotion of great delight or happiness." (dictionary.com.) The *Thesaurus* gives "happiness" as a synonym for "joy." But what brings "happiness" varies from one person to the next, and from culture to culture, making "happiness" a rather ambiguous term. And happiness itself can be elusive.

The Coca-Cola Company has an ad: "Coke: open happiness." Does the thrill of opening a coke on a scorching day "open happiness"? Maybe. But it's momentary. If happiness were a bottle of pop being opened, then everyone should be happy!

Happiness is associated with "things" to make a pitch to you, the consumer. A new wardrobe will bring you happiness. A new car will bring you happiness. A house will bring you happiness. A boat will bring you happiness. The list gets longer and longer, but the sad day comes. The wardrobe gets old. The car gets old. The house begins to need repairs. And they say the two happiest days are when a man gets a new boat and the day that he gets rid of it!

Ponder these questions:

What is it that brings you happiness?

What is it that brings you **joy unspeakable**?

Happiness is an emotional experience. We all share this emotion, some more than others. But what is that unshakeable joy, that joy that is unwavering? This book is about that eternal joy, that Kingdom joy, that **joy unspeakable**. It's the joy that comes from knowing the One True God, Yahweh.

If you think it is a narrow-minded statement to say that only believers can know eternal joy, please let me explain. This is not to say that non-believers cannot know pleasure or happiness on this earth, but that they cannot abide in eternal Kingdom joy.

Please listen to the words of Christ:

"Enter by the narrow gate. For the gate is wide and the way is easy that leads to destruction, and those who enter by it are many. For the gate is narrow and the way is hard that leads to life, and those who find it are few." Matthew 7:13-14

The New Living paraphrase puts it this way: "You can enter God's Kingdom only through the narrow gate. The highway to hell is broad, and its gate is wide for the many who choose that way."

Jesus Christ, the prophesied Messiah, God incarnate, is that narrow gate. He said, "I am the way, and the truth, and the life. No one comes to the Father except through Me." John 14:6

How true these lyrics ring! John Newton wrote these words in the hymn "Glorious Things of Thee Are Spoken."

"Solemn joys and lasting treasures, none but Zion's children know."

Zion is a reference to God's Kingdom. Only those who trust in God can know eternal **JOY!**

"GLORIOUS THINGS"

John Newton, famed for his "Amazing Grace" lyrics, wrote the words of this 18th-century hymn. "Glorious Things of Thee Are Spoken" speaks of the glories of Zion, God's City.

PSALM 87

1 On the holy mount stands the city He founded;
2 the LORD loves the gates of Zion
more than all the dwelling places of Jacob.
3 Glorious things of you are spoken,
O city of God. Selah.

The music is set to the tune of Franz Joseph Haydn. Later, this glorious music was desecrated with the words "Deutschland über Alles" of the Third Reich, a counterfeit of God's Kingdom, a kingdom of antichrist. Let us re-take this music back for the glory of God!

"The thief comes only to steal and kill and destroy. I came that they may have life and have it abundantly." John 10:10

THE SOURCE IS YHWH

*"Glorious things of you are spoken,
O city of God. Selah."* Psalm 87:3

Great and mighty things are said of the people of God, the people who know YHWH and their "source of joy" is in Him.

"Singers and dancers alike will say, "My whole source of joy is in you." Psalm 87:7 (Holman Christian Standard)

The source of the LORD is joy unspeakable. The joy of the LORD is His absolute favor, His redemption, His glorious workings. Our source is YHWH. The root of joy is wholly His.

"Then singers, as they play their instruments, will declare,
"All my roots are in you."
Psalm 87:7 (International Standard Version)

Our root is in the LORD. Our source is from Him. Root, source, or spring, it's all the same thing. It grows out and blossoms out as the "fruits of the spirit."

Therefore, when we don't see "joy" manifesting in our lives, we must go down to that root of Jesus Christ. Jesus Christ is our source of all joy, all love, all righteousness, and all peace.

> "For the kingdom of God is ... righteousness and peace and joy in the Holy Spirit." Romans 14:17

I pray you'll find this treasure.

> "May the God of hope fill you with all **JOY** and peace in believing, so that by the power of the Holy Spirit you may abound in hope." Romans 15:13

Let your hope and **JOY** well up!

ON JOY AND HAPPINESS

Everyone wants to be happy.... or do they? Some people seem content in their misery, perhaps fearful of change. But generally, it seems most people thirst for happiness.

Nowadays, there is a field of study called "positive psychology." Positive psychology deals with studying emotions such as happiness and joy. Psychology, as can be seen in its name, deals with matters of the "psuche" or soul.

This branch of psychology has found that happiness varies in different cultures. Happiness is therefore very subjective.

"Happiness is the meaning and the purpose of life, the whole aim and end of human existence." ~ Aristotle

If happiness is an emotion, then was Aristotle saying that the whole aim and end of human existence is an emotion? Probably not. Aristotle's definition of happiness, "eudaimonia" in the Greek, included a striving for excellence and a purposeful life. Yet even a purposeful life, a purpose-driven life, will not necessarily yield the joy of knowing Christ. Aristotle knew not Christ and His joy. The philosopher's version of happiness, although lofty, is centered in the realm of the soul. The joy of the LORD bubbles up from the spirit.

While the soul's happiness is subjective, perhaps one could say the opposite about the joy of the LORD. In a sense, it is objective. There is only one Source of this joy. The object of our adoration, the LORD Himself, is our joy! The joy of the LORD is in the spirit realm. Yet it does also overwhelm and encompass the soul, rapturing it upward into the spirit realm! Then the two, the soul and the spirit, are agreed.

The LORD "changes not" and therefore, the spiritual joy we have from Him changes not, but remains constant within us. However, just as we are not always focused on the LORD's Spirit within us and with us, we are not always accessing the joy we have from His Presence. Yet we have the right to go freely enjoy His Presence anytime and into His JOY.

ON THE SOUL AND THE SPIRIT

There is a debate among Christian scholars about whether or not the soul and the spirit are the same thing. It was years before I was even aware of this debate. To me the Scripture plainly makes a distinction between spirit and soul.

"Now may the God of peace Himself sanctify you completely, and may your whole spirit and soul and body be kept blameless at the coming of our Lord Jesus Christ." 1 Thessalonians 5:23

Indeed, the words "spirit" and "soul" in both the Greek and the Hebrew are different words. "Psuche" (G5590) and "nephesh" (H5315 נֶפֶשׁ) translate to "soul." "Pneuma" (G4151) and "ruach" (H7307 רוּחַ) are the words for "spirit", either also being translated as "wind."

There is a difference between the spirit and the soul. There is a vast qualitative contrast between the merriment of the soul and the joy of the spirit. Yet, admittedly, the soul and the spirit are intertwined, so much so that we have this truth:

"For the word of God is living and active, sharper than any two-edged sword, piercing to the division of soul and of spirit, of joints and of marrow, and discerning the thoughts and intentions of the heart." Hebrews 4:12

"So sharp and quick sighted, and so penetrating is the divine Word, that it reaches the most secret and hidden things of men ..." (Gill's Exposition of the Entire Bible)

The soul is rather apparent. When you're happy, you're happy. Unless you are hiding your sentiments. Someone can cleverly disguise the facade of fake emotions, but those who are aware of the telltale signs are not fooled. "The Mentalist", from the TV series, was able to deduce matters that someone not as witty as himself might not have caught.

But as to the spirit, it's a different ball game.

"The spiritual person judges all things, but is himself to be judged by no one." 1 Corinthians 2:15

Our spirits are "hidden with Christ" (Colossians 3:3) and known totally only to God.

"The Christian's life is lodged in the sphere of 'the unseen and eternal.'" *Pulpit Commentary*

"The natural person does not accept the things of the Spirit of God, for they are folly to him, and he is not able to understand them because they are spiritually discerned." 1 Corinthians 2:14

"The natural man. The Greek word is ψυχικὸς (psychical); literally, soulish, i.e. the man who lives the mere life of his lower understanding, the unspiritual, sensuous, and egoistic man. He may be superior to the fleshly, sensual, or carnal man, who lives only the life of the body (σωματικὸς); but is far below the spiritual man (πνευματικός)." *Pulpit Commentary*

"Far below the spiritual man." Definitely!

"The natural man, the wise man of the world, receives not the things of the Spirit of God. The pride of carnal reasoning is really as much opposed to spirituality, as the basest sensuality. The sanctified mind discerns the real beauties of holiness, but the power of discerning and judging about common and natural things is not lost." *Matthew Henry's Concise Commentary*

The spirit of man can be discerned by the Spirit of God working in us, but the fruit is perceived! The fruit of the Spirit is our manifestation. Joy is amongst them.

Additionally, we need to not judge[1] the spirits for their souls have not yet "caught up" with their new man, the inner man! Our spirits are perfect!

"You therefore must be perfect, as your heavenly Father is perfect." Matthew 5:48

We are perfect if we are walking in the Spirit! The spirit doesn't sin!

Now, the spirit can be utterly joyful *inside* because our Source is constant and peerless. We look at the LORD Jesus Christ whose passion was before Him:

"And He said to them, 'My soul is very sorrowful, even to death.'" Mark 14:34a

---

1 See article on "Judgment or Reproof?" for fuller explanation. http://hisinheritance.org/2010/05/11/judgment-or-reproof/

How can it be that He was sorrowful *in the soul* and yet "for the joy that was set before Him endured the cross"? (Hebrews 12:2) He was downcast *in the soul* and yet He had the SPIRITUAL DELIGHT to know His death would bring about the deliverance of the many.

One outwardly may be in dire circumstances and not exhibiting any suggestions of bliss, but the **JOY** of the spirit rings through!

A NEW SPIRIT

Without the Word of God living in one's heart, perhaps there is not a great need for a distinction between soulish happiness and spiritual joy. Yet, once one is born-again, we should offer the distinction.

Jesus answered, "Truly, truly, I say to you, unless one is born of water and the Spirit, he cannot enter the kingdom of God. That which is born of the flesh is flesh, and that which is **born of the Spirit is spirit.** Do not marvel that I said to you, 'You must be born again.' The wind blows where it wishes, and you hear its sound, but you do not know where it comes from or where it goes. So it is with everyone who is born of the Spirit." John 3:5-8

If we are "born again of the Spirit", a deeper joy is evident. A new spirit is God's promise to believers through the prophet Ezekiel:

"And I will give you a new heart, and a new spirit I will put within you. And I will remove the heart of stone from your flesh and give you a heart of flesh." Ezekiel 36:26

We need a new spirit, because the old spirit died, died to God when we first sinned. The concept of death in Hebrew thinking was that of separation. Sin separates our spirits from the spirit of God. We are brought back, reconciled to God in Christ, the bridge between our heart and the heart of God. Christ is the only way back to union with the Spirit of God.

"For through Him [Jesus Christ], we both [Jews and Gentiles] have access in one Spirit to the Father." Ephesians 2:18

Christ, Emmanuel, "God with us", did this because He loved us so!

"Who gave Himself for our sins to deliver us from the present evil age, according to the will of our God and Father." Galatians 1:4

He became the Lamb of God slain from the foundations of the world for our sins. He is our salvation!

"Yet I will rejoice in the LORD; I will take **JOY** in the God of my salvation." Habakkuk 3:18

RENEW YOUR MIND

We get a new spirit, but on the other hand, we do not get a new soul! Believers still have the same mind, though it is now in the process of being renewed. We have also the mind of Christ in us! But we still have our aptitudes and attitudes, some which may need to be submitted to the will of God. We still may enjoy the same foods, the same hobbies, but the Holy Spirit in us will lead us more and more away from illicit pleasures. Old habits unbecoming saints will need to be broken, but this is a process and a work of His Holy Spirit in us. Our personalities may be the same, but now enhanced. Our emotions may still be similar, but may need to be submitted. Our soul - mind, will and emotions—all three need to be renewed.

"Do not be conformed to this world, but be transformed by the renewal of **your mind**, that by testing you may discern what is the will of God, what is good and acceptable and perfect." Romans 12:2

"He saved us, not because of works done by us in righteousness, but according to His own mercy, by the washing of regeneration and renewal of the Holy Spirit," Titus 3:5

"The washing of regeneration and renewal of the Holy Spirit" is the work the Spirit does within us, renewing our minds, often referred to as the process of sanctification.

"Conversion and sanctification are the renewing of the mind; a change, not of the substance, but of the qualities of the soul. The progress of sanctification, dying to sin more and more, and living to righteousness more and more, is the carrying on this renewing work, till it is perfected in glory. The great enemy to this renewal is, conformity to this world. Take heed of forming plans for happiness, as though it lay in the things of this world, which soon pass away. Do not fall in with the customs of those who walk in the lusts of the flesh, and mind earthly things. The work of the Holy Ghost first begins in the understanding, and is carried on to the will, affections, and conversation, till there is a change of the whole man into the likeness of God, in knowledge, righteousness, and true holiness. Thus, to be godly, is to give up ourselves to God." *Matthew Henry Commentary*

So we see in these Scriptures and this exegesis, we are encouraged to be renewed in our mind. It is a new spirit that enables us to do so. The soul should be subordinate to the spirit.

The Scriptures urge us to "walk in the Spirit", **not** to walk in the soul! (Which seems to me to indicate a definite distinction between the spirit and soul, as regards that argument!)

"But I say, walk by the Spirit, and you will not gratify the desires of the flesh." Galatians 5:16

"And I will put my Spirit within you, and cause you to walk in my statutes and be careful to obey my rules." Ezekiel 36:27

"There is therefore now no condemnation to those who are in Christ Jesus, who don't walk according to the flesh, but according to the Spirit." Romans 8:1 WEB

We Christians are to be Spirit-led, not driven by the soul, our own purposes and plans, or carnality.

The idea of the Spirit-led life is that we walk in the spirit which is one with the Spirit of God, submitted to the will and word of God. Our souls should be submitted under our spirit which is submitted to and in union with Christ. Our bodies should be submitted under our souls.

"But we are not people who shrink back and perish, but are among those who believe and **gain possession of their souls.**" Hebrews 10:39 WNT

We who are born again of the Spirit should **possess** our souls! In other words, keep them in line!

Thus, we should have this order of authority in our life:

1. **The Holy Spirit of Christ**

2. The **new spirit** in Christ

3. The **soul** in the process of sanctification to become like Christ

4. The **body**

It is easy to see how there is trouble when this hierarchy is upside-down. When one lets the body rule one's life, one gives in to the sinful lusts of the flesh.

"And you were dead [separated from the life of God] in the trespasses and sins in which you once walked, following the course of this world, following the prince of the power of the air, the spirit that is now at work in the sons of disobedience among whom we all once lived in the passions of our flesh, carrying out the desires of the body and the mind, and were by nature children of wrath, like the rest of mankind." Ephesians 2:1-3

That foul spirit is demonic and we once followed along in wicked ways. We all were once out of order! We all were disobedient to God and "carrying out the desires of the body and the mind."

"The acts of the flesh are obvious: sexual immorality, impurity and debauchery; idolatry and witchcraft; hatred, discord, jealousy, fits of rage, selfish ambition, dissensions, factions and envy; drunkenness, orgies, and the like. I warn you, as I did before, that those who live like this will not inherit the kingdom of God." Galatians 5:19-21

We now need to be walking in the Spirit.

"But the fruit of the Spirit is love, joy, peace, forbearance, kindness, goodness, faithfulness, gentleness and self-control. Against such things there is no law. Those who belong to Christ Jesus have crucified the flesh with its passions and desires. Since we live by the Spirit, let us keep in step with the Spirit." Galatians 5:22-24

And in that fruit is **JOY!**

THE CARNAL MIND

"For the mind that is set on the flesh is hostile to God, for it does not submit to God's law; indeed, it cannot." Romans 8:7

Well-educated unbelievers ruled by the prowess of their prideful minds may find it difficult to admit their disobedience and sinfulness. At least many addicts, those ruled by the flesh, admit their guilt which is a needed step towards repentance and deliverance. The intellectual unbeliever, on the other hand, may see no need for repentance, not even acknowledging their Creator. Society feeds their pride. Civilization may scorn the drug addict or the sexually perverse but still hold in honor the intellects, though they be godless atheists. Yet, today, society has declined so low to the point of even condoning, some even glorifying deviant behavior! This downward spiral, the Scriptures teach, begins with denying their Creator.

"For this reason, God gave them up to dishonorable passions." Romans 1:26

The intellects too can have their own perversions where they allow the body to control their lives rather than aspiring to God's image and plan for humankind. Just look at all the scandals exposed in the news of supposedly "respectable" people, even confessing Christians! If one is not careful to be "walking in the Spirit", we become more susceptible to the seductions of the flesh.

There is another path followed by many unrepentant proud intellectuals. It is the path of "enlightenment." This poison is served up in many pleasant flavors: Buddhism, New Age, Masonry, and Mormonism. These various paths, however, all converge on a devious downslope to hell. They all promote the oldest lie in the book: "you will be like God."

"'You will not certainly die,' the serpent said to the woman. 'For God knows that when you eat from it your eyes will be opened, and you will be like God, knowing good and evil.' When the woman saw that the fruit of the tree was good for food and pleasing to the eye, and also desirable for gaining wisdom, she took some and ate it. She also gave some to her husband, who was with her, and he ate it." Genesis 3:4-6

It is the proud mind that wants to be God in the sense of deciding for oneself what is right and what is wrong. Yes, the fruit from the Tree of the Knowledge of Good and Evil looks good but it is poison. Only the Sovereign Creator YHWH who made heaven and earth has the right to say what is evil and what is good. He reserves His right to set the rules in His Kingdom. It is not unjust or unreasonable for Him to deny access to the rebellious:

"Outside are the dogs and sorcerers and the sexually immoral and murderers and idolaters, and everyone who loves and practices falsehood." Revelation 22:15

In His Word, God has defined "magic arts", sexually immoral acts, idolatry and other sins. We don't get to rewrite the rules in His Kingdom. Those who are unrepentant and refuse God's authority and His Way of salvation have chosen their own way which won't get them into His

Kingdom. They have chosen the Tree of the Knowledge of Good and Evil instead of the Tree of Life, Jesus Christ. The unrepentant will never know Christ and His Kingdom joy.

"'Behold, I am coming soon, bringing my recompense with me, to repay each one for what he has done. I am the Alpha and the Omega, the first and the last, the beginning and the end. Blessed are those who wash their robes, so that they may have the right to the tree of life and that they may enter the city by the gates.'" Revelation 22:12-14

Those who eat from the Tree of Life will know **JOY** beyond measure!

PETER'S REBUKE

It's not only the bullheaded that are carnally minded. We all have that tendency. Peter was rebuked by Jesus.

"Get behind me, Satan! You are a hindrance to me. For you are not setting your mind on the things of God, but on the things of man." Matthew 16:23

I wonder how Peter felt at that rebuke! But then the LORD goes on to invite him to follow Him.

"Then Jesus said to His disciples, 'If any one desires to come after Me, let him deny himself and take up his cross and follow Me.'" Matthew 16:24 (DBT)

This translation uses the verb "desires" which is in the original Greek. Now, thinking about this, there seems to be a conundrum. On one hand, Christ is speaking to a "desire" and on the other hand, "deny" would imply that you're not doing what you want! So which is it?

Paul explained this in Romans 7. Or I should say he attempted to explain this, as it sounds quite confusing if one does not rightly divide the "I"s!

"For I do not understand my own actions. For I do not do what I want, but I do the very thing I hate." Romans 7:15

Here Paul is showing how there is a war for our soul between the spirit and the flesh! This battle has often been pictured in cartoons with a little devil whispering in one ear and an angel whispering in the other. In reality, the born-again spirit draws the soul to the things of God while the flesh pulls it towards wickedness.

Paul continues, "For I have the desire to do what is right." v.18

That desire is springing from his born-again spirit! We need to walk in the spirit and do the things our spirit desires because our spirit is in the Holy Spirit of God!

Paul continues, "Now if I do what I do not want, it is no longer I who do it, but sin that dwells within me." v. 20

To clarify, let's read it such:

"Now if I [in my carnality decide with my soul to] do what I [in my spirit] do not want, it is no longer I [in my spirit] who do it, but sin that dwells within me [my flesh]."

So we see the struggle for the soul of man. But your new spirit is already seated in heavenly places!

Paul concludes with this:

"22 For I delight in the law of God, in my inner being, 23 but I see in my members another law waging war against the law of my mind and making me captive to the law of sin that dwells in my members. 24 **Wretched man that I am!** Who will deliver me from this body of death? 25 Thanks be to God through Jesus Christ our Lord! So then, I myself serve the law of God with my mind [his renewed mind], but with my flesh I serve the law of sin."

"Wretched" is the opposite of "joyous." But there is **JOY** in walking in the Spirit and doing the desires of the Spirit!

DYING AND DELIGHT

You may wonder what a discussion on the soul and the spirit has to do with joy. If one does not live as God intended, one cannot have the joy that God has promised.

"'There is no peace,' says my God, 'for the wicked.'" Isaiah 57:21

The cravings of the flesh never end. It is the fallen nature of the beast. Therefore, a Christian must "die daily" to the flesh. We must practice "walking in the Spirit."

"So you also must consider yourselves dead to sin and alive to God in Christ Jesus." Romans 6:11

Let us walk in the Spirit! If we walk in the Spirit, we will die to sin. In the Spirit, we can delight in the LORD!

"Delight yourself in the LORD, and He will give you the desires of your heart." Psalm 37:4

I believe this is a double-entendre. If you delight yourself in the LORD, you will ultimately change your desires! Now your desires are His wishes! His desire is for you, and you are His desire!

"Whom have I in heaven but You? And there is nothing on earth that I desire besides You." Psalm 73:25

Yet God has a strange way of aiming you to be who you were intended to be!

"For I know the plans I have for you, declares the LORD, plans for welfare and not for evil, to give you a future and a hope." Jeremiah 29:11

Some of the things I've desired were ideal for who God was making me. Even a long time ago, God was shaping me for my destiny. I wasn't aware at that time that God had a purpose for my life!

I learned French back in high school. Years later I had the opportunity of doing that camp in France. My visit there was so much more meaningful.

I've been a travel agent. That was training for me to do mission trips.

I had a desire to be a teacher. I later taught my children, some who were homeschooled at various points, and taught a class on geography at a Christian school part-time. I taught piano.

I had a desire to write. I have a blog for children, blog for my lyrics and a blog for my walk with Christ.

I had the desire to lead worship. I've sung for many years. I lead people to the throne room of God.

Years ago, I expressed a desire to see the "treasury of snow."

"Have you entered into the treasury of the snow?" Job 38:22 KJ2000

Just in passing, I mentioned it to the LORD. Over time, I had forgotten. Well, one day on my Alaskan cruise, I saw it. The Spirit reminded me of my request. Praise God! He brought me here! The wonderful "treasury of snow", the glaciers in Glacier Bay National Park, was a sight to behold. What an absolutely beautiful world the LORD has created for us!

"He fulfills the desire of those who fear Him; He also hears their cry and saves them." Psalm 145:19

But all in all, the LORD will be faithful to bring us to the place of perfect peace!

"But the meek shall inherit the land and delight themselves in abundant peace." Psalm 37:11

And there we will have unspeakable **JOY!**

HOW TO DIE DAILY

"I have been crucified with Christ. It is no longer I who live, but Christ who lives in me. And the life I now live in the flesh I live by faith in the Son of God, who loved me and gave Himself for me." Galatians 2:20

"And those who belong to Christ Jesus have crucified the flesh with its passions and desires." Galatians 5:24

The Apostle Paul wrote, *"I die daily."* (1 Corinthians 15:31)

Die daily? "What does that mean?" I pondered. How does one die daily?

Did Paul die daily? Certainly, he had to make daily decisions to continue in the difficult call God had on his life despite the threat of death. Yes, he was often in danger and peril of physical death. Yes, he "fought with wild beasts" and was shipwrecked and beaten. But do you have to be a martyr to "die daily"?

In our own day, many Christians worldwide must choose to remain faithful in the face of death. May the LORD grant them the grace and courage to echo Paul!

"As it is, my eager expectation and hope that I will not be at all ashamed, but that with full courage now as always Christ will be honored in my body, whether by life or by death. For to me to live is Christ, and to die is gain." Philippians 1:20-21

My own experience is certainly not comparable to either Paul's or martyrs' trials. Yet, I have had to "die" to my fear and do God's will in the face of the possibility of danger, possibly death.

I had been invited to a meeting between Christian and Islamic leaders while overseas. I felt God had brought me to such a place for such a time. But a church had just been burnt down by terrorists in another town not far. There was unrest in the land. A meeting was called between the religious leaders. I was invited along by a local pastor. Oh, the questions that went through my head! Would they kidnap me? Would they murder me? I was obviously an American. That night, I prayed fervently and put my life in the hands of My LORD. I died to self and submitted my will to the will of the LORD. So I went the next day, come what may. At the meeting, I stood out as a foreigner with my light brown hair and blue eyes, but I sat down and prayed in the Spirit the whole time. Thankfully, there was a good outcome. The leaders were able to come to some kind of agreement and the local turmoil subsided. No church was burned in that town, in the meantime. And I was safe. Praise God!

That was dying to self. But there are less extreme examples. Some of these are mundane, but they qualify for "die daily."

* Dying to self is closing one's mouth when one wants to respond in anger to insults.

* Dying to self is getting up out of bed and blessing the baby that is screaming for attention.

* Dying to self isn't cursing the driver who just cut you off.

* Dying to self is not taking the extra bill the cashier just gave you in your change.

* Dying to self is simply telling your flesh to be still!

A good friend of mine does it this way. When she recognizes the ugly carnal nature rising up in rebellion, she says, "Shut up, Carnita!"

But the above examples were all about subduing undesirable emotions. Sometimes we are also called to die to something much bigger, maybe even a long-term aspiration.

But lest all this talk about dying depress you, let's look at the flip-side! Dying to self is, actually, for the Christian, living to God!

"So you also must consider yourselves dead to sin and alive to God in Christ Jesus." Romans 6:11

The flip side is joy.

There is a kid's song sung to the "Jingle Bells" melody. "Joy" in those Christian lyrics is defined as:

"J-O-Y! J-O-Y! This is what it means:

Jesus first, yourself last and others in between."

So simple. So upside down is worldly thinking from God's ways! The key to happiness and joy is not doing whatever you have a-hankering to do, but doing what God intended you to do. You need to be who He created you to be! In His will, there is **JOY!**

THE #1 JOY SAPPER

UNFORGIVENESS

"And forgive us our sins, for we ourselves forgive everyone who is indebted to us." Luke 11:4

Unforgiveness. What a joy sapper! What a thief! Unforgiveness steals joy, makes one bitter, eats away at one's health, and gives you extra wrinkles and gray hair! Why hold on to it? Let it go!

Forgiveness is a decision, an act of your will. Your born-again spirit man in you holds NO unforgiveness. Unforgiveness is in the flesh and the unsubmitted parts of your soul.

Therefore, choose to forgive.

But one may protest again, "I don't feel like forgiving! I can't help how I feel!" Oh, really? Then one is allowing emotions to rule one's life. Feelings have usurped authority. Feelings are sitting on the throne of the heart and have booted God off! Those negative emotions are unsubmitted to God. They need to be put in their proper place.

Or perhaps one is even more defiant against God's command to forgive, and declares, "I will NOT forgive!" In this area then, the will is not surrendered to the will of the Father. But Christ taught us to pray to Our Father, "Thy will be done." One must forgive to have joy!

Jesus told the parable of an unforgiving servant:

"Then his master summoned him and said to him, 'You wicked servant! I forgave you all that debt because you pleaded with me. And should not you have had mercy on your fellow servant, as I had mercy on you?' And in anger his master delivered him to the jailers, until he should pay all his debt. So also my heavenly Father will do to every one of you, if you do not forgive your brother from your heart." Matthew 18:32-35

The word for jailers above is also translated "one who tortures" and "tormentors."

Jailers keep one imprisoned. Unforgiveness keeps one imprisoned in hateful thoughts, ill will and negative emotions. Unforgiveness is a tormentor! And there's no **JOY** in that!

THE REMEDY FOR UNFORGIVENESS

Here is the remedy for unforgiveness: Walk in the Spirit. The fruit of the Spirit is love.

"Above all, keep loving one another earnestly, since love covers a multitude of sins." 1 Peter 4:8

Practically, here are some actions that one could take to banish unforgiveness:

Confess to God one's sin of unforgiveness. Tell God how you feel! King David did. Pray that He changes your heart.

Choose to forgive as an act of obedience to God Almighty who requires it. Choose! This is aligning your soul with the will of God. Your spirit already wants to forgive!

Pray for help from the Holy Spirit and read Scriptures to renew your mind.

Pray for the person who wronged you. Pray that God's will be done in his life. Pray God's best for that person's life. Prayer is an expression of good will for someone. Good will is the opposite of ill will. By an act of sheer obedience in praying for someone who has wronged you, you will in effect be submitting your will under God's will.

"Bless those who curse you, pray for those who abuse you." Luke 6:28

Once you have chosen to do God's will, chose to forgive and walk by faith. Those feelings and wrong mindsets will fall in line under your spirit's will, which *is submitted* to God's will.

God is for us, not against us. But He calls us to repentance for any unforgiveness which is in defiance of God's law of love. Repentance is a decision of your will. It's worth repeating: **Repentance is a decision of your will.** Make a decision with *your will* to obey God and forgive. Your feelings, your emotions, will line up afterward with the decision of your will. Don't continue to let this negative emotion steal your **JOY**.

"Again I say to you, if two of you agree on earth about anything they ask, it will be done for them by my Father in heaven." Matthew 18:19

Let's take a very spiritual application of this Scripture.

The new born-again spirit in a believer IS in union with the Spirit of God and is therefore of the same mind of Christ. But the soul (mind, will, and emotions) is in the process of sanctification, being conformed and transformed until that Day when He appears and we shall be like Him!

So, your spirit is right. It's already seated in heavenly places with Christ Jesus. Your natural man needs to come into agreement with your spirit and the Holy Spirit! It's decision time again. Tell yourself, "I will forgive because God tells me to!" Consciously make Scriptural decisions by your will. Here you are bringing your soul into agreement with your spirit.

Sometimes the mind wanders. But I can **choose** to get in a posture of prayer and so that agreement helps to bring my mind into a holy place, too. When I don't "feel" like being joyful, I can choose to dance before the LORD, and the joy deep down in my heart springs forth.

I will be joyful because He instructs, "Rejoice in the LORD always." Philippians 4:4

God has given us free will. We have a free will to make choices. But He encourages us through the words He spoke through His Prophet Moses to "choose life!"

"I call heaven and earth to witness against you today, that I have set before you life and death, blessing and curse. Therefore, choose life, that you and your offspring may live, loving the LORD your God, obeying His voice and holding fast to Him, for He is your life...." Deuteronomy 30:19-20

We have a choice between life in Christ or death, between the blessings of obedience or the curses that come through disobedience. We have a choice between the bondage of unforgiveness OR the freedom in forgiveness. We have a choice between doing things our loving Father's way or our own selfish way. We have a choice between the temporary "pleasures" of this world and the **JOY of the LORD.**

A WORLD FULL OF JOY

PURSUIT OF HAPPINESS

The temporary "pleasures" of this world, if immoral, stand in contrast to the **JOY** of the LORD. They don't hold a candle. But what of the pursuit of happiness? Are we not to pursue happiness as Christians? These are the profound words of America's founding document, the Declaration of Independence:

> "We hold these truths to be self-evident, that all men are created equal, that they are endowed by their Creator with certain unalienable Rights, that among these are Life, Liberty and the **pursuit of Happiness**.--That to secure these rights, Governments are instituted among Men, deriving their just powers from the consent of the governed, --That whenever any Form of Government becomes destructive of these ends, it is the Right of the People to alter or to abolish it, and to institute new Government, laying its foundation on such principles and organizing its powers in such form, as to them shall seem most likely to effect their Safety and Happiness.
>
> Signed in Congress, July 4th, 1776" (Emphasis mine)

The Founding Fathers of our country saw fit to include "the pursuit of Happiness" as a right endowed by their Creator. Yet if one forgets their Creator, they may have passing pleasure and momentary carnal happiness but they will not have true joy!

The Pilgrims pursued their happiness all the way across the Atlantic! They endured many natural hardships in their new land in that "pursuit of Happiness." They pursued the freedom to worship the One True God of Abraham, Isaac and Jacob, according to His Holy Word and His ideals. This was true liberty!

The history of both this country and the Church abounds with stories of those who knew the greatest joy of knowing Jesus Christ. They risked all else for the pearl of great price - His Kingdom!

So we may freely pursue our happiness, with respect to other's rights and happiness and with respect to the Creator's laws. God's laws were always intended for the "general Welfare" of the people. The "general Welfare" of the people was also a foremost priority in the establishing of America, as seen in the Preamble to the Constitution:

"We the People of the United States, in Order to form a more perfect Union, establish Justice, insure domestic Tranquility, provide for the common defense, promote the general Welfare, and secure the Blessings of Liberty to ourselves and our Posterity, do ordain and establish this Constitution for the United States of America."

How then are we perverting the Constitution nowadays to allow for the condoning of perversions and sin? As people are seduced away from their Creator in this once free nation, they move away from their liberties and His blessings.

"Now the Lord is the Spirit, and where the Spirit of the Lord is, there is freedom." 2 Corinthians 3:17

The liberty we are guaranteed by the Constitution, which was "endowed" to us by our Creator could not include licentiousness and depravities. Licentiousness does not work for the "general Welfare." True liberty in Christ is freedom from sin, not a license to sin.

"For you were called to freedom, brothers. Only do not use your freedom as an opportunity for the flesh, but through love serve one another." Galatians 5:13

God had kept America mainly hidden for centuries, waiting for the day when His saints would need a place to flee the political and religious corruption of the European continent. It is a haven for those seeking freedom and their "pursuit of Happiness." Sadly, the sins of the many are seeking to destroy liberty.

May we encourage them in the knowledge of Christ, where true liberty and joy is found. May America remain a promised land abounding in the **JOY of the LORD** as her strength!

COMMON JOYS

God's plan for mankind has always intended liberty and happiness! In His goodness, YHWH-Shalom led the Pilgrims to America. In His goodness, YHWH-Yireh led Abraham to the Promised Land of Israel. In His goodness, Elohim placed man in the beginning in the Garden of Eden, in paradise where joy in His Presence was abundant. But mankind had fallen from grace and strayed from our Creator. In His goodness, His plan is to bring us back to paradise and joy beyond our greatest earthly happiness.

Yet even in this fallen world, God has gifts of great **JOY** along the way.

BABIES!

"When a woman is giving birth, she has sorrow because her hour has come, but when she has delivered the baby, she no longer remembers the anguish, for joy that a human being has been born into the world." John 16:21

The birth of a child is a time to celebrate and brings happiness to both believers and non-believers. As a Granny, I have eight grandchildren!

We had two adoptions in our family. What a joy to see the happy faces of the children.

"He gives the barren woman a home, making her the joyous mother of children. Praise the LORD!" Psalm 113:9

How much greater our **JOY**, though, knowing that a baby is gift from God, not just a biological consequence! How much greater our **JOY**, knowing that we have been given the responsibility of nurturing a child in the ways of holiness and Godliness!

GOD'S GOODNESS IS JOY

Our heavenly Father is so good. There are joys to be shared by all humanity.

"For He makes His sun rise on the evil and on the good, and sends rain on the just and on the unjust." Matthew 5:45

"Every good gift and every perfect gift is from above, coming down from the Father of lights with whom there is no variation or shadow due to change." James 1:17

Common events that bring happiness to most people are compounded when a spiritual dimension is added. COMMON HAPPINESS COMPOUNDED = JOY

The early Church had joy in the seemingly mundane!

"And day by day, attending the temple together and breaking bread in their homes, they received their food with glad and generous hearts." Acts 2:46

Let us find that **JOY** in the simple things, with a grateful heart for life and breath and scrumptious food!

CONTINUALLY FILLED

"49 And the word of the Lord was spreading throughout the whole region. 50 But the Jews incited the devout women of high standing and the leading men of the city, stirred up persecution against Paul and Barnabas, and drove them out of their district. 51 But they shook off the dust from their feet against them and went

to Iconium. *52 And the disciples were filled with joy and with the Holy Spirit."* Acts 13

The verb, "were filled", in the Greek shows continuous action. So another translation points that out in the last line:

"And the disciples were continually filled with joy and with the Holy Spirit." (NASB)

Wouldn't you like to be continually filled with joy? That joy comes with the empowering of the Holy Spirit! Whenever I am filled with the Holy Spirit, except for times of intercession, I am also filled with joy! Joy and the Holy Spirit go hand in hand!

Reading the above passage, we find that the Apostles had just been driven out of town! Were they down in the mouth about it! No! "They shook off the dust from their feet" and carried on in the LORD's work

If we are doing what the Lord has called us to do, there should be joy in that - a continual joy! It's a continuous **JOY** of knowing what you're called to do and doing it.

CLIPPER

Years ago, when I had the honor of leading worship for a mission trip abroad on my first mission trip, an elderly lady walked up to me and expressed her appreciation for my ministry. Then she said that the LORD had given her a wonderful ministry, too. Curious, I asked her about it. She stated, "I clip toenails for people in nursing homes." I will never forget her words and humility. Years later, I remember the joy on her face as she spoke those words. Those of us who have platform ministries should never forget that our LORD also washed the feet of His disciples. Some of the most intense precious **joyous** times I've shared with the LORD have been in service to the broken.

INDIA

The last place in all the earth I wanted to go was India. I had heard the distress was so great that I wouldn't be able to bear the poor and the wretched. As an intercessor, I imagined myself walking around and crying all day! But when the time came, I went, figuring it was better to get this thing over with.

My room in the hotel, the only one in the area, was horrid. I had to ask for new sheets for the bugs were so rampant. The blanket I threw on the side. I took a dry bug wipe to cover the poles of my bed so that nothing could creep up. The bed liner was filthy, so I took a baby wipe to get some of the dirt off. I slept in my raincoat that night in dread of insects.

There was one little thing - actually, it wasn't so little: a huge spider. It was almost the size of the palm of my hand! I didn't know what to do. I finally took the trash can and caught the creepy thing!

I cried, "Oh LORD, what am I doing here?" Well, the Presence of the LORD just came in an unusual way. For the whole time in India, I experienced His Presence. I just enjoyed His Presence. It took my mind off the dinginess. The grasshoppers at the outdoor stage didn't bug me.

What impressed me so was that the Christians of India were joyful! They had so little material goods but they were happy. They sat on the floor at meetings, but they were happy. They were happy to be serving God.

These disciples, in the above stories, were serving the Kingdom. They were serving and therein is **JOY!**

THE JOY OF CREATION

"He is the Maker of heaven and earth, the sea, and everything in them-- he remains faithful forever." Psalm 146:6

We were eating al fresco one evening at a lakeside restaurant in Canyon Lake, Texas. As the sun began to set, the guests put their forks down and just stared at the sky before them. People one by one stood to attention and began applauding, as the sunset grew even more dramatic. The diners came from inside the restaurant to see what the excitement was all about. They, too, stood and clapped. It was the most spectacular sunset I had ever witnessed. I gave the glory to God the Creator of heaven and earth.

Maybe scientists see it as a feat of nature. But we as Christians know that although there is a science behind such beautiful sunsets, there is firstly a Creator who fixed the sun in the sky and the made the atmosphere such as it is to bless us with wonderful sights to behold. And we as Christians know that is it is God who orders our steps to put us in that place of beauty at just the right time and the right place. It was a gift from God and we give Him thanks. God has so blessed my life with the joy of witnessing great beauty. Actually, that awareness of God's goodness compounded the joy of that sunset! Those who are not thankful have a less intense happiness. Thankfulness is a source of **JOY!**

DAILY GIFTS

Buying yourself something special is a treat that brings happiness. But the joy is deeper and more special when your husband figures out what would make you happy and surprises you with that wonderful gift! I love good chocolate. But I seldom buy it for myself. My husband buys it. It makes it more special because it comes from a heart of love.

Our heavenly Father bestows on us daily gifts because He loves us. Being aware of His love yields a greater joy! Yet the sunsets, the bird songs, and the fragrant flowers are there for all to enjoy. Sadly, not everyone takes the moment to stop and smell the roses.

Those who do, and those who are thankful, have joy. Grateful people are happy people. The converse is true also.

Ungrateful people tend to be unhappy complainers. But we can train ourselves to be thankful.

My almost daily confession and declaration of thanksgiving is:

"Blessed the LORD, oh my soul, who daily loads me with blessings!"

That is a personalization of the psalm:

"Blessed be the Lord, who daily loads us with benefits, even the God of our salvation. Selah." Psalm 68:19 (AKJ)

It's a great way to start the day! "Lord, what are we going to do today? I know you have something good in store for me!"

His Presence is itself enough, which we believers can enjoy daily no matter the circumstances. So my daily blessing doesn't have to be some mountaintop high. It can be the **JOY** of a simple flower.

IN THE BEAUTY OF THE IRIS

This story was written back in 1993 and I've had these little blooms of delight annually!

"Now unto Him who is able to do exceedingly abundantly above all we ask or think, according to the power that works in us, unto Him be glory in the church by Christ Jesus throughout all generations, forever and ever. Amen." Ephesians 3:20

The ladies' retreat had been refreshing. We were filled to overflowing with heavenly manna, but I still had one tiny, frivolous wish: to win a door prize. How lovely one of those purple silk flower centerpieces would look in my living room with its plush, amethyst carpet! Oh, where was my name tag to place in the drawing?

I searched all my packed bags at least twice to no avail. The raffle went on without my name. C'est la vie! No chance for me. But I was genuinely happy when the guest who had come with us won! After all, God knows who needs a blessing most. Perhaps it was a real encouragement to our guest. But then the Lord blessed us all. The scenic ride home through the Texas countryside displayed God's creative genius in a colorful profusion of spring flowers. I went to bed that night quite happy, even though I hadn't won the purple door prize.

Yet, the Lover of my soul had heard my prayer! Little did I know the delight He had planned especially for me. The next morning, I walked outside my home. Something beautiful had occurred during the night. There on my front lawn, all over my lawn, the most wonderful, little purple flowers had sprung up! My lawn was like a wildflower meadow! I stooped to pick one up and suddenly sensed in the depth of my heart the Lord's still small voice. He whispered gently, "This is your live bouquet!"

Tears welled in my eyes as God's love overwhelmed me. Isn't it just like our Lord to answer prayers "above all that we ask"? I had requested a small artificial bouquet and instead He had lavished on me a yard full of vibrant, living irises that bloom each and every spring! And they were all my favorite color purple!

I was so taken by this romantic gesture of the Lord that I decided to research my flower. None of my neighbors' yards boasted this particular beauty. Yet on mine, they seemed to be just springing up out of the St. Augustine grass. I actually thought my grass was blooming! The stems of the flowers were similar to the blades of grass. But an expert on grass assured me that St. Augustine could not bloom. So I went to the library and found a book on Texas wildflowers.

This particular wild iris was dubbed "Herbatia." The petite bloom had three main petals, each not much bigger than a thumbnail. I thought how the three petals could represent the three-in-one, triune God. But I saw more symbolism in this fragile flower: it could represent how fleeting is mortal life. Its official nickname was "Celestial" due to its ephemeral existence. An individual iris has a total lifespan of only seven hours! Its petals unfold about ten in the morning and they close about five in the evening. The next day a new batch will unfurl, but each individual flower is so very transient. Yet the Creator chose to pack all this delicate beauty into this teeny flower that lives for a mere seven hours! Such a speck in time!

This short-lived masterpiece reminds me of our Savior's words: "Consider the lilies... even Solomon in all his glory was not arrayed like one of these! If then God so clothes the grass... how much more you?" Luke 12:27-28

And just how does the Lord clothe us? He clothes us in His righteousness and His holiness. His glory will arise on us and be seen upon us! (Isaiah 60:1-2)

Not only are we so clothed but we smell good too! Even better than a rose! "For we are the aroma of Christ." Through us, He "spreads everywhere the fragrance of the knowledge of Him." We are "the fragrance of life", Christ's life in us! That's why the devils are disturbed by our mere presence – we smell like Christ! To the devils, that is the smell of their inevitable demise! Dear saint, never underestimate the power of Christ in you! Even your smell – the fragrance of Christ in you – makes the enemy cringe! (See 2 Corinthians 2:14-16)

My prayer is that whenever we smell the fragrance of a rose, or behold the fleeting glory of a lily in full bloom, or enjoy the ephemeral beauty of a Celestial iris, we will remember and appreciate the Lord's promise to His church, His bride: we will be forever arrayed in the fine splendor of His glory!

"That He might make known the riches of His glory on the vessels of mercy, which He had prepared beforehand for glory…." (Romans 9:23)

"But we all… beholding as in a glass the glory of the Lord, are changed into the same image from glory to glory…" (2 Cor 3:18)

"When Christ who is our life appears, then you will also appear with Him in glory." (Colossians 3:4)

"Beloved, now we are the sons of God, and it does not yet appear what we shall be: but we know that when He shall appear, we shall be like Him; for we shall see Him as He is." (1 John 3:2) O glorious Day!

Now every spring, I am greeted with this "Celestial" perennial reminder that our life here will fade just as the flowers. But in the beauty of the iris, I also see His promise that our good Lord does "exceedingly abundantly above all that we can imagine"! So when our frail life here fades, we will be transported into His eternal glory! HalleluYAH! **JOY!**

MY HAPPIEST TIMES

It will not surprise you that some of my happiest moments were my wedding day and the births of my children and more recently the births of my grandchildren. What can compare with love and life? Mankind has been blessed as a whole with these wonderful experiences, all due to a gracious God who ordained marriage and family.

What are some of my most cherished memories?

What joy to finally know the Savior of mankind! My encounter in the spirit with Jesus Christ transformed my life and left me "walking on air" for weeks.

What joy to dance in the spirit with the Lover of my soul, Jesus Christ!

What joy to wake up in the morning with a touch from the LORD!

What joy to lead someone to the Truth of Jesus Christ!

What joy to be instantaneously healed!

What joy to have a prayer answered!

What joy to have a "desire of your heart" fulfilled without asking!

What joy to feel the Presence of the LORD!

What joy to know the approval of your heavenly Father!

What joy to hear that your Redeemer loves you!

What joy to have the Holy Spirit within you bursting forth in prayer and praise!

These are joys that unbelievers know not. Take a moment to recall your memories with the LORD and be thankful for His lovingkindness. Give Him praise!

"Because Thy lovingkindness is better than life, my lips shall praise Thee." Psalm 63:3

Now that should have brought joy bubbling up! Praise Him for the happy times! Praise Him through the sad times as they'll work out for good! Praise Him for the joy down in your heart! Praise Him for the everlasting joy!

"He will wipe away every tear from their eyes, and death shall be no more, neither shall there be mourning, nor crying, nor pain anymore, for the former things have passed away." Revelation 21:4

No more pain and sorrow! All **JOY!**

JOY IN THE JOURNEY

There's **JOY** in the journey! I've referenced before the camp that we did for the children of Chernobyl. Preparing for that camp was for me like Abraham's journey to the Promised Land. I say this not to compare myself to the patriarch of great faith but to show how we can learn from the lives of saints who went before us. God has supernatural journeys for those who respond to His call!

Like Abraham's journey, mine began with exact direction from the LORD. The LORD gave me a dream or vision one morning. I saw in the spirit a map of a lake and an "X." It marked a near-shoreline location. Somehow He communicated to me that this was "Camp Holiness" (not its real name but its designation for God's purposes) where I was to do a camp for the children of Chernobyl. Somehow I just knew in the spirit this camp was located in western France, but there were no names to indicate its exact location. Little did I know the great adventure that the LORD would lead this Texas gal on to get me there!

Like Abraham perhaps, I had no prior thoughts of packing up and going off on such a journey when the LORD called. This was something totally out of the blue! But often God calls His saints to do things that seem totally out of their comfort zone. Abraham had to move to a far-off place. Gideon had to lead a fight for which he felt ill-prepared. Peter the fisherman became the leader of the Church in Jerusalem. Truly, "Who is sufficient for these things?" (2

Corinthians 2:16) So, to God be the glory! He was taking me for a Holy Spirit ride!

I had no prior experience whatsoever in doing children's camps. I had never even been to a children's summer camp! When my family went camping on the river, my preference was a motel room, if possible. And I hadn't even taught Sunday School! My only related experience was when my children were young, I had once written and directed a Vacation Bible School at a very small church. My main ministry since my recommitment to Christ had always been in the choir and singing solos. What did I know about doing a camp, let alone one in France? With children brought from the Chernobyl area?! Wouldn't that involve government red tape?

I admitted to the LORD that I didn't even know where to begin. Yet, I also yielded to His will and agreed to do it, if He would get me started.

So the LORD led me step by step, miracle by miracle, and then one day, a friend and I left to find this camp somewhere in France. The last day before we needed to leave for home, I went into a tourist board, and lo and behold, there was a relief map like the one in my dream! I just pointed to the spot where the "X" had been in the dream and inquired about that camp. Incidentally, it was numbered "7", a number often associated with God!

So my friend, who had a lot of experience with children's camps, and I proceeded to the camp to check it out. "It's perfect!" my friend exclaimed and pointed out all the advantages. We were ecstatic and filled with **JOY!**

STEALING THE JOY

Then out of nowhere, the enemy swooped in. I was not prepared for this attack, which came in the form of a physical disorder of my friend. The enemy tried to steal our joy just at the moment of victory! I guess he was quite livid. After all, this camp could be an extreme blessing and change many lives!

I was confused for a moment by the attack, but then, by the grace of God, I realized the enemy had come to steal my joy! I determined not to be dismayed. My friend soon regained her norm, and we went back to Texas with memories of a grand adventure, both in the natural and supernatural!

The point being here in this anecdote is that the enemy will try to steal our joy!

The camp was planned for the next summer. We hosted seventeen little girls ages about eight to ten for three weeks there in that camp in Gerardmer, France. It was a glorious time! We did crafts and danced to praise music and hiked in the mountains. Our daily Bible lessons were about the fruit of the Spirit.

But another time there at the camp, the enemy tried to steal my joy. It was a comment made with good intentions, but nonetheless, it threw me off my equilibrium for a little bit. Don't let the enemy steal your **JOY!**

PUSHING BUTTONS

We all have weak spots. The enemy of our soul knows exactly where those weak spots are. He knows how to push our buttons just to irk us.

My weak spot is I'm overweight. I've been chubby all my life but I'm also a large-boned woman with a size 10 1/2 shoe! However, it's an area of sensitivity.

A very wonderful and kind doctor came to the camp to help us. She freely examined all our children and bought them needed medicines with her own money. We met her on our first trip. She was eating in a restaurant all alone. She looked a little awkward when we were first seated. I asked her to join us because I could speak a little French. As it came out in the conversation that we were to do a camp for the children of Belarus, she committed herself to see them. God was working this out for me, too. I had a doctor for my first camp!

But she made a remark to me about how I needed to take care of myself first, in regards to my weight. I don't remember what I said to her, but I know I didn't respond in anger. However, I was crushed. I cried. I confided in Lisa, the other camp counselor and my sister in the LORD. She consoled me and prayed for me and got me back to my cheery self. I couldn't be depressed with so many children here with much bigger problems! Writing this now, it sounds a bit wimpy on my part.

Anyway, I won't give space to excuses or reasons on my weight. I am normally healthy, praise God! People in France don't seem to have weight problems, so they don't understand it. Of course, the French cooks refuse to use inferior food and use real butter, real cheese and fresh produce in all their cooking. Up there in the mountains of Gerardmer, walking around, and eating three gourmet meals a day with French bread and chocolate every day for a snack, I actually lost a pound a week! Who'd guess?! The wholesome air and really *good* food helped!

But I do have a victory in this arena to report. Have I dropped a lot of weight? After my last hospital stay, I did lose some weight. No, I'm still a large woman in the natural but in the spirit, I'm a "lean, mean fighting machine" against the forces of hell! But here in lies my **JOY** and victory!

THAT BUTTON DOESN'T WORK NO MORE!

The camp was in 1999 when the enemy pushed that button. In 2014, I went on a fantastic mission trip to Israel with my church.

The LORD had directed my Pastor to pray in Samaria where the LORD had ministered to the woman at the well. (John 4)

I had the connections in Israel as this was my fifth trip to the Holy Land. We met a local pastor at the well in Nablus. We also spontaneously sang there at the well with another Christian group visiting. It was a holy moment singing "Alleluia!" with other saints where Jesus had ministered.

And then the enemy decided he would swoop in like he had in the past in our moment of victory to try to steal my joy. He pushed that same button again. This time, he used a member of the Orthodox clergy at that church. Didn't the enemy use the Apostle Peter to try to dissuade Christ from the cross? Jesus replied, "Get behind me, Satan!" So, if the devil can use Peter, he can use anyone if we're not careful! Anyone not walking in the Spirit, at the moment, can be used to speak a discouraging word by the enemy. James warns us against the tongue's destructive potential:

"But no human being can tame the tongue. It is a restless evil, full of deadly poison. With it we bless our Lord and Father, and with it we curse people who are made in the likeness of God. From the same mouth come blessing and cursing. My brothers, these things ought not to be so." James 3:8-10

He writes "no human being can tame the tongue." So are we without hope in that area? Far from it! The Spirit of God in us *can* tame the tongue! That's why we need to walk in the Spirit! If you lash out at someone in the flesh, be assured you are not walking in the Spirit at that moment. However, the Spirit can use someone to give a hard word, a rebuke, or a correction but this is something about which one should be very sure. I have often heard people say, "I have a word for you" when it is obviously only their own opinion! If the LORD truly gives a word of correction, it comes with the hope and empowerment for transformation, not the criticism of condemnation.

"A gentle tongue is a tree of life, but perverseness in it breaks the spirit." Proverbs 15:4

Have you ever received a correction from the LORD Himself? Once I remarked, "I'm a jack-of-all-trades, master of none." The LORD quickly rebuked me never to say that. He Himself was making me into a master of those talents which He had placed in me. I obeyed and was thankful for His correction and never said that of myself again! God's word came with the hope that He was changing me from glory to glory.

So getting back to my story, this very thin priest at the church in Nablus came out and commented to me, without any kind of greeting, and hardly knowing any English, "You eat too much." Now, I never would have imagined a priest could say something so abruptly and rudely to a complete stranger!

Anyway, I was so in the Spirit, and so filled with the joy of the LORD, this fiery dart missed its target! I actually laughed about it, not to his face but to myself, recognizing the same ploy of the enemy and knowing I had yet another victory! Ha! Ha!

Again, my point being, that the enemy comes to steal your joy.

"But know this, that if the master of the house had known in what part of the night the thief was coming, he would have stayed awake and would not have let his house be broken into." (Matthew 24:43)

If you know the thief will come to steal your **JOY**, be forewarned and ready!

THE THIEF

Since the **JOY** of the LORD is our strength, is it any wonder that the devil wants to steal that joy? One day I was despairing and I heard distinctly in the spirit the LORD advise me, "Tell the devil he can't steal your joy!" Well, I knew it was the voice of my LORD, so I said it out loud.

"Devil, you can't steal my joy!" And then I said it louder, "Devil, you can't steal my joy!"

Now, this is a tactic that I've used many times since.

Some people want to walk all over us, if we let them. So does the devil.

"The thief comes only to steal and kill and destroy. I came that they may have life and have it abundantly." John 10:10

When the thief comes to steal your joy, just say "No!"

"No!" is a powerful word. Self-defense experts assert that yelling a bold "No!" at an attacker is a first-line defense.

Everyone hesitates for a split-second when they hear a loud "No!"

But the devil won't give up all that easily. Make it plain to him that you mean business! Practically, that means start praising the LORD! Or start singing or dancing. Or quoting Scripture.

"Submit yourselves therefore to God. Resist the devil, and he will flee from you." James 4:7

*"...they shall obtain gladness and **JOY**, and sorrow and sighing shall flee away."*
Isaiah 51:11

OTHER JOY SAPPERS

There are many things in life that can sap one's joy, one's strength. Some of the experiences are unavoidable and just part of life.

The death of a loved one is hard on the soul and emotions. A holy Jesus wept at the death of Lazarus. But there was joy at the lad's resurrection!

There is "a time to weep, and a time to laugh; a time to mourn, and a time to dance." Ecclesiastes 3:4

Christians are not called to be stoics. We are not to be callous or unfeeling. Emotions are part of our soul and God made them. Jesus wept and the Holy Spirit can be grieved.

"Is anyone among you suffering? Let him pray. Is anyone cheerful? Let him sing praise." James 5:13

If one is spiritually healthy, these periods of mourning are not eternal.

"Weeping may last for the night, But a shout of joy comes in the morning." Psalm 30:5 NASV

However, there are bad habits we may have acquired that can turn into joy sappers. Since the joy of the LORD is our strength, they sap our strength as well. Here are some common ones:

Too little time with God. Our strength comes from the LORD. We need to be in His Word and Presence.

Too much negative news. Know how much you need to know and how much you can handle without it sapping your joy. This may vary from individual to individual. It may also depend on other factors in your life. Intercessors watch the news to know how to pray, but we need to be careful not to get overloaded. Of course, praying through the burden and giving it back to the LORD, will take the burden off you. Know your limits. The rate of negative news coming at us through the media in these dark times can easily "wear down the saints." (Daniel 7:25)

Too much negativity from friends and family. We are to be salt and light but sometimes we need to pull back from hanging out with negative people. We need the company of saints full of faith so that we can minister to our negative friends, not let them pull us down. Jesus withdrew to be refreshed by the Father.

Stress and overload. Sometimes we need to say "No!" to friends and family and activities that overload our schedules. We need to have a weekly rest. This is not the norm in American culture. Perhaps we need to reassess our priorities from a Scriptural perspective if we find ourselves constantly overloaded. God is not overloaded that He finds Himself huffing and puffing. We can all take time for a break. Our bodies need a rest! Oh saints, it is so important for us to rest!

"And He said to them, "Come away by yourselves to a desolate place and rest a while." For many were coming and going, and they had no leisure even to eat." Mark 6:31

Fatigue and sickness. Again, these are conditions common to humanity. They can take a toll on one's joy, one's faith, one's strength. Even a cold can put us out of commission for a bit. A cold means one's defense is down. A good way to avoid it is to keep a saline solution for up the nose!

At times like these, we need the Body of Christ to stand with us. Yes, you DO need to be in a community of loving believers! We help one another and when we need help, they are there for us. We don't have to fight battles alone.

"... so that you too may have fellowship with us; and indeed our fellowship is with the Father and with his Son Jesus Christ. And we are writing these things so that our **JOY** may be complete." 1 John 1:3b-4

JOYFUL, JOYFUL

Our desire is to be joyful and keep the joy-sappers at bay. Instead of getting all negative, try doing this:

Christian Music. Listening to Christian music brings joy to my soul! While working and during mundane matters, it can soothe one's soul and spirit. The antidote to stress may be good Christian radio!

"... but be filled with the Spirit, addressing one another in psalms and hymns and spiritual songs, singing and making melody to the Lord with your heart" Ephesians 5:18-19

If your place of work doesn't allow Christian music, calming music will be best.

"Don't worry! Be happy!" The world sings that cheerful phrase. Sometimes that just ignores the problem, but it's better than fretting yourself into a heart attack. Christ has the solution!

Casting your cares on Him. Give it to Jesus!

"Humble yourselves, therefore, under the mighty hand of God so that at the proper time He may exalt you, casting all your anxieties on Him, because He cares for you." 1 Peter 5:6-7

"Cast your burden on the LORD, and He will sustain you; He will never permit the righteous to be moved." Psalm 55:22

How do you cast your cares on the Lord? Give your problems to the LORD and leave them with Him. It is sometimes easier said than done.

I've seen this done in a church service. It is a prophetic act that can help. People were encouraged to write their problems on a piece of paper and put it on the altar at church. You can do this anywhere, anytime. You don't need a physical altar, just the altar of your heart. Now crumble up the paper with your list of problems and throw it to the LORD! "Here, LORD, catch!"

We have the privilege of going boldly to our Father with our concerns.

"So let us keep on coming boldly to the throne of grace, so that we may obtain mercy and find grace to help us in our time of need." Hebrews 4:16 ISV

*"But I will sing of Your strength and will **JOYFULLY** proclaim Your faithful love in the morning. For You have been a stronghold for me, a refuge in my day of trouble."*
Psalm 59:16

LOSING MY STRENGTH

When I was about 50 years old, I was ill for an extended time. I was too weak, from loss of blood, to do much but lie around. The Scriptures proclaim the "life is in the blood" and I knew that experientially because I could feel my life draining from me. I grew weaker and weaker. All those things that I knew to stay in a place of joy, I couldn't do physically. I couldn't dance. I couldn't sing for long. Reading was even sometimes difficult. I quoted healing Scriptures, but at some point, I tired of the fight. I wanted to just give up and die. I told the LORD if He wasn't going to heal me, to just take me home.

Oh, but thank God for His saints! When we are weak, He is strong on our behalf. He works through His people. The prayers and support of family and church and the faithfulness of God brought me through.

Through this time, there were joys along the way. It is a joy for a mother who has ministered for many years to her children to see the fruit of that labor. When I needed a word of encouragement in my sickness, my grown son David gave me a Scripture, that which the LORD Himself spoke to Paul:

"My grace is sufficient for you, for My power is made perfect in weakness." 2 Corinthians 12:9

That word really encouraged me. And it encouraged me more that it came from my own son!

It really is a joy to see your children grow up responsibly in the LORD. All my children have been a blessing to me.

"A wise son [and daughter] brings JOY to his" mother!

Proverbs 10:1

"THE BEST IS YET TO COME"

The specialists could not figure out what was wrong with me. One visit it was one disease, another it was something else. It was a lot of speculation. Anyway, they told me I would be taking the "little purple pill" for the rest of my life!

"Wait, a minute!" I thought. I remembered the Scripture that God heals ALL my diseases. Oh, it's so beneficial to have the Word of God stored up in your heart! I suggest you go through the psalms and the book of Mark and highlight healing Scriptures so you have them when you need them!

"Bless the LORD, O my soul, and forget not all his benefits, who forgives all your iniquity, who heals all your diseases…" Psalm 103:2-3

I asked the doctor, "Are you telling me this can't be healed?" Well, that's what he thought! Didn't God's Word say differently? Whose report would I believe?

I stood on the Word of God. Now, God does work through doctors and medicine, but these doctors were telling me I would not be healed. And that was not acceptable to me.

But I had a relapse and ended up back in the hospital. This time, the doctor told me my colon was so bad that he would have to cut out some of it. He didn't tell me that that could mean I had a bag attached to me for the rest of my life. Not a good prognosis at all.

But thank God for the saints! A nurse came in to see me and prayed for me. Then she sent in the chaplain. He prayed and stated, "The best is yet to come!" It resonated as the Truth of God in my whole being. My spirit recognized God speaking a direct word to me through this man. And if God speaks something to you, and you recognize it as the voice of God, you can take that word to the bank!

So I didn't have that operation. Obviously, that was not "the best"!

All the visions and words that the LORD had given me over the years had not yet come to pass. How could they if I were sickly? I felt akin to the woman with the issue of blood, (Luke 8) but I was confident there would be healing and JOY in this, too.

SPIRIT, SOUL, AND BODY

"Therefore, take up the whole armor of God, that you may be able to withstand in the evil day, and having done all, to stand firm." Ephesians 6:13

Now, sometimes God can work a complete supernatural miracle. He once healed my back instantaneously and two days later I was riding a roller coaster!

But since we are spirit beings with souls and bodies, we need to deal with those areas also. We need to be uplifted in our souls and renewed in our minds. We need to eat healthfully and give our body the nutrients it needs, generally.

God made our bodies to heal themselves. I am not a doctor but some things are obvious. Cuts heal. Pulled muscles with rest restore. Our immune systems fight off infections.

Many physical conditions are due to a lack of nutrients. I remembered learning how limes had been effective in alleviating scurvy from sailors many years ago. I remembered how some natural honey recommended by a country vendor had almost immediately cured the coughing condition my son had had for weeks which medicines had not helped.

The following is not medical advice. It is my personal story of spirit, soul, and body. God's Words on healing and His Spirit encouraged me in faith for healing. I attacked my problem from a spiritual perspective. I used my mind and did the research and gained knowledge of my problem with the help of the internet. I took care of my body dealing with the physical reality.

Often we don't get the best solution to our problems because we deal with them only from a one-sided approach when we need a three-sided approach: spirit, soul, and body! If we don't deal with spiritual roots of a problem or negative mindsets, how can one expect a permanent solution? Had I not had the Word of God on the matter, I would have listened to the negative prognosis of the doctors who were not men of faith. And my problem would not have been solved until heaven!

I was determined to overcome this problem with faith and practicality! I stood on the Words in Scripture and the specific word God had given me: "The best is yet to come."

To God be the glory! Even though this wasn't a supernatural healing, He gave me the Word of hope!

I thank my friends who stood with me in the fight with their prayers and support. I took a little retreat with some friends to rest during that time of illness. I prayed and wrote some songs to my Savior. I kept my spirits up with the Word and with remembering all that God had already done for me - all the good times. I found a photo album with the words "Life is good" embossed on the cover. I bought it and filled it with memories of good times and looked at it whenever my spirit was waning. I thanked God for those blessed times. And I thanked Him for His promise of "the best" to come!

I was confident that I would be healed. No "little purple pill" for the rest of my life for me! I weaned myself off that medicine. My family doctor, who had always been very accommodating to my distaste for pharmaceuticals, gave me a little insight. He told me the cortisone with which I was being treated was the synthetic of a hormone made naturally by the body. So I took a nutrient for adrenal glands from time to time when under stress. I basically had no problems for ten years.

The next ten years, the LORD had chock-full! My children were married and had grand babies! I went on mission trips that included Costa Rica, Nicaragua, Belarus, India, and last but not least, Israel. We had some major vacations which included New Zealand and Alaska. I even did a life-long dream of mine and had a singing part in the "The Sound of Music."

Oh, my life was full and I was full of **JOY!**

CHANGE MY HEART

All throughout those ten years, I had no more than a common cold, and that was only when I didn't have the nasal spray!

But the most wonderful thing happened when I got sick the second time. God used it to change my heart.

There was some hurt in my heart and it had been causing me to have wicked thoughts about someone. Yes, wicked. Our flesh is wicked. We must will to obliterate those sentiments. We must decide to cast down those wicked thoughts. But it is a battle and I had cried out to the LORD to change my heart in this matter. It was murderous. For didn't our LORD compare anger to murder?

"You have heard that it was said to those of old, 'You shall not murder; and whoever murders will be liable to judgment.' But I say to you that everyone who is angry with his brother will be liable to judgment." Matthew 5:21-22a

I knew I needed to eradicate these thoughts, but how? Paul knew this dilemma. Every saint has a sin nature that must be kept under Spirit-control. We must die to the flesh and its carnal nature daily.

"But I see in my members another law waging war against the law of my mind ["reasoning" G3563] and making me captive to the law of sin that dwells in my members. Wretched man that I am! Who will deliver me from this body of death? Thanks be to God through Jesus Christ our Lord! So then, I myself serve the law of God with my mind ["reasoning" G3563], but with my flesh, I serve the law of sin." Romans 7:23-25

"We destroy arguments and every lofty opinion raised against the knowledge of God, and take every thought captive to obey Christ." 2 Corinthians 10:5

I cried out to the LORD for help.

This same person who had unknowingly caused me that inner pain had also been changed by the LORD's grace, and now spoke to me comfort and words that wiped away the old hurt. So, once again God was working for my good, in the midst of a bad situation! Glory to God! I am so thankful that God changed my heart - again! He molds us and makes us and changes us from glory to glory as we behold Him! Now, that is a reason for great **JOY!**

God wants us to win. Sometimes if we don't pass a test, we have to re-take it!

"As for me, I shall behold your face in righteousness; when I awake, I shall be satisfied with your likeness." Psalm 17:15

"Beloved, we are God's children now, and what we will be has not yet appeared; but we know that when He appears we shall be like Him, because we shall see Him as He is." 1 John 3:2

In the midst of trials, we can know that God is molding us into His holy image. There is **JOY** in that assurance.

THANKFULNESS

THANKFULNESS

My life has been so blessed and I am truly thankful. Thankfulness is a wonderful restorer of joy. I am blessed with His Presence! That is enough! But besides which, God has truly given me desires of my heart and a wonderful family and friends. Whenever I look back over my life, especially since I began walking with the LORD, mine has been a phenomenal one! Even the hard times beforehand, He has turned for my good.

Everyone can be thankful for something. If you're feeling a bit blue, make a list of those things for which you are thankful. Thank God for those things and give Him praise. There's no room for depression when one is giving thanks! True thankfulness will blossom into joy. And if you don't feel like giving thanks, remember Christians are not called to walk by their feelings. Give thanks **by faith**! Just do it! That obedience to "give thanks" will work in you.

After all, no matter what is happening this day in your life, could it be any worse than what our LORD endured for us? Yet, He gave thanks at the time of His impending suffering!

*"… for the **JOY** that was set before Him [He] endured the cross …"*

Hebrews 12:2b

PSALM 118

Psalm 118 is the last of a group of hymns called the "Hallel" or praise psalms that were traditionally sung or recited at Passover. Christ, knowing His suffering, crucifixion and death were imminent, nonetheless would have joined with His disciples at that Last Supper Passover to give thanks!

"Oh give thanks to the LORD, for He is good; for His steadfast love endures forever!" Psalm 118:1

"I thank You that you have answered me and have become my salvation." Psalm 118:21

"This is the day that the LORD has made; let us rejoice and be glad in it." Psalm 118:24

Yes, Christ was giving thanks for that day, even with the knowledge of the next day's cross! Thanks be to God for such a Savior and example! Christ also knew by faith that God would work that dark day of the LORD's death out for eternal good! So our Passover Lamb gave thanks!

"This is the day that Lord Jehovah has made; come, we will leap for JOY and rejoice in Him!"

Psalm 118:24 (Aramaic)

DAIYENU

"... but rejoice that your names are written in heaven." Luke 10:20

"It would have been enough!" That's the meaning of "Daiyenu", a chipper little ancient ditty of thanksgiving sung traditionally at Passover for over a thousand years.

There are 15 verses. Each recounts an event from the Jew's Exodus out of Egypt for which they give thanks to God. But even just the event of the first verse is enough reason to give thanks.

"If He had brought us out of Egypt, it would have been enough!"

Amen to that! What a great song to inspire us to thankfulness and joy! You can look up the song on the internet and learn to sing it. I sing it frequently, especially when I'm waxing sad, to remind myself that the Passover Lamb is enough!

"One of the primary purposes of the Passover Seder is to make us feel as if we personally experienced the exodus from Egypt and the redemption from slavery to freedom." [2]

Praise God! Each true Christian has personally experienced an exodus and redemption from the slavery and

---

[2] *("What Does 'Dayenu' Mean Today?" by Joshua Ratner on "My Jewish Learning" http://www.myjewishlearning.com/blog/rabbis-without-borders/2014/04/01/what-does-dayenu-mean-today/)*

bondage of sin into the freedom of Christ! That is enough! That is enough for which be eternally thankful!

"Thanks be to God for his inexpressible gift!" 2 Corinthians 9:15

Jesus Christ is the gift of God to us! Yet, Christ has done so abundantly more for us! He's given us the **Source of JOY!**

THE JOY OF SALVATION

"Yet I will rejoice in the LORD;
I will take JOY in the God of my salvation."
Habakkuk 3:18

We are called by His name only if and because we have been redeemed by the precious blood of the Lamb! Therefore, we rejoice!

Our salvation is a cause of great joy! And His name is Salvation!

"I, I am the LORD, and besides Me there is no Savior." Isaiah 43:11

Some false brands of religion claim to be "Christian" yet deny that Jesus Christ is God! That is not Scriptural. Jesus Christ declared Himself to be God and God declared that there is no Savior besides Him!

"And there is no other god besides Me, a righteous God and a Savior; there is none besides Me. Turn to me and be saved, all the ends of the earth! For I am God, and there is no other." Isaiah 45:21-22

In Chapter 45 alone, God declares over and over again, six times, that there is no other true God besides Him! (Verses 5, 6, 18, two times in 21, 22) He wanted to be sure we understood the point!

There is no other name but the name of Jesus: "YAHshua", "YAH saves", the name "I AM salvation!" They all mean the same! "YAH is salvation!"

"Behold, God is my salvation; I will trust, and will not be afraid; for the LORD GOD is my strength and my song, and He has become my salvation. With **JOY,** you will draw water from the wells of salvation." Isaiah 12:2-3

If you're not presently drawing that living water up from the well of salvation, then pray as the psalmist David did:

"Restore to me the **JOY** of your salvation, and uphold me with a willing spirit." Psalm 51:12

Believers have the right to pull up that joy from their well of salvation anytime. Let us remember the joy of our salvation!

"But may all who seek you **rejoice and be glad in you**; may those who love your salvation say continually, 'Great is the LORD!'" Psalm 40:16

You can make a choice, a decision to be thankful and joyful for your salvation! Declare it:

"I will **greatly rejoice** in the LORD; my soul shall exult in my God, for He has clothed me with the garments of salvation." Isaiah 61:10

And so shall the shouts of joy resound:

"Shouts of **joy and victory** resound in the tents of the righteous: "The LORD's right hand has done mighty things!" Psalm 118:15 (NIV)

And the LORD Himself delights in His people whom He has redeemed. He sings over us!

"The LORD your God is in your midst, a mighty One who will save; He will **rejoice** over you with gladness; He will quiet you by His love; He will exult over you with loud singing." Zephaniah 3:17

"For the LORD takes pleasure in His people; He adorns the humble with salvation." Psalm 149:4

Here is the first verse of the song I wrote based on the above Scripture, expressing joy in His salvation.

"Rejoice! Rejoice! In our Lord's exaltation! Children of Zion, be **joyful** in our King! He beautifies the humble with salvation. Saints, be joyful in glory and sing!"

Yes, let us rejoice because we are saints, redeemed by the blood of the Lamb!

"Yet I will rejoice in the LORD; I will take **JOY** in the God of my salvation."

Even Mary, who gave birth to the Messiah, rejoiced in her salvation and Savior, in the words known now as "The Magnificat":

"And Mary said, 'My soul magnifies the Lord, and my spirit **rejoices** in God my Savior, for He has looked on the humble estate of His servant. For behold, from now on all generations will call me blessed.'" Luke 1:46-48

Mary, the mother of the Anointed One, had great **JOY** in Her Savior!

"FOR THE JOY SET BEFORE HIM"

*"… looking to Jesus, the founder and perfecter of our faith, who for the **JOY** that was set before Him endured the cross, despising the shame, and is seated at the right hand of the throne of God. Consider Him who endured from sinners such hostility against Himself, so that you may not grow weary or fainthearted."*
Hebrews 12:2-3

Ah, sweet Jesus!

"The joy set before Him" was the salvation of everyone who would believe, from the time of Adam to the last saint in the Kingdom.

"The joy set before Him" was redeeming us from the throes of evil and Satan's nasty legions.

"The joy set before Him" was translating us "to the kingdom of His beloved Son." Colossians 1:13

"The joy set before Him" was to fill us with His divine Holy Spirit.

"The joy set before Him" was "granting an inheritance to those who love me, and filling their treasuries." Proverbs 8:21

"The joy set before Him" was to make us like Himself!

"The joy set before Him" was to have us all in His Kingdom "of righteousness and peace and **JOY** in the Holy Spirit."

Joy! Joy! **JOY!**

THE JOYS OF THE KINGDOM

SPIRITUAL BLESSINGS

Christ has so blessed us!

"Blessed be the God and Father of our Lord Jesus Christ, who has blessed us in Christ with every spiritual blessing in the heavenly places, even as He chose us in Him before the foundation of the world, that we should be holy and blameless before Him. In love, He predestined us for adoption as sons through Jesus Christ, according to the purpose of His will, to the praise of His glorious grace, with which He has blessed us in the Beloved. In Him, we have redemption through His blood, the forgiveness of our trespasses, according to the riches of His grace, which he lavished upon us…." Ephesians 1:3-8

God has truly lavished His blessings upon us!

Our Savior said: "I came that they may have life and have it abundantly." John 10:10

Yes, we serve a big God who is a lavish Giver and does not do things in mediocrity. He granted us eternal life to all who would believe on His name!

"He who did not spare His own Son but gave Him up for us all, how will He not also with Him graciously give us all things?" Romans 8:32

And so what good thing will He withhold?

"Fear not, little flock, for it is your Father's good pleasure to give you the **kingdom**." Luke 12:32

"Therefore, let us be grateful for **receiving a kingdom** that cannot be shaken, and thus let us offer to God acceptable worship, with reverence and awe." Hebrews 12:28

Receiving a Kingdom is pure **JOY!**

SAINTS IN THE KINGDOM

We saints are spiritually in God's Kingdom already!

"He has delivered us from the domain of darkness and transferred us to the kingdom of His beloved Son." Colossians 1:13

He has transferred us *already*!

"And raised us up with Him and seated us with Him in the heavenly places in Christ Jesus ..." Ephesians 2:6

Your two feet may be on the earth, but **your spirit** is in the Spirit of Christ in the heavenly realm.

Where is your soul? Perhaps if it is watching a television show it, too, is in the earthly realm. But if you are meditating wholly on the things of God, your soul is raptured upwards to the heavens. Conceivably this is why people receive so many visions during worship and times of fasting.

So we are encouraged,

"If then you have been raised with Christ, seek the things that are above, where Christ is, seated at the right hand of

God. Set your minds on things that are above, not on things that are on earth." Colossians 3:1-2

The things of earth are in no way comparable to the **JOYS** of heaven.

JOY IS A JEWEL

Ah, the treasures that have been lavished upon us who believe in Christ. We have been blessed "with all spiritual blessings." Joy is a jewel amongst those blessings. Grab it! Grasp it! Delight in it! It is yours! Joy is a gift from your Heavenly Father, freely bestowed.

Joy is a jewel. Be adorned with His joy as with priceless jewels! Smile and be happy in the midst of a dreary world.

"For the kingdom of God is not a matter of eating and drinking, but of righteousness and peace and joy in the Holy Spirit." Romans 14:17

Joy is a jewel. It is a facet of the Kingdom of heaven, a facet that shimmers. We ARE His jewels, made to sparkle in the Light of His glory and grace!

The righteous people are marked by facets of joy and peace. On the other hand, those never in the Kingdom, are self-righteous, stubborn and dour. Interestingly, "dour" is a word that comes from a Scottish Gaelic root that could mean "dull." Whereas, some Hebrew words for "joy" come from roots meaning "bright." We are made to be bright jewels shining in His Kingdom!

Do you have joy? Yes, yes, yes, you do - if you are in Christ! As a Christian, you already have joy! But are you in the habit of accessing that joy that is available to you? Or are you still stuck in the mud that the world has thrown at you?

Christ "said, 'The kingdom of God comes not with observation: Neither shall they say, 'See here!' or, 'See there!' for, behold, the kingdom of God is within you." Luke 17:20-21 (AKJ)

Do you believe Jesus' words that "the kingdom of God is within you" - His kingdom "of righteousness and peace and joy in the Holy Spirit"? Joy is a facet of that Kingdom and therefore, joy, too is within you, inside of you!

We believers live in a fallen world with troubles and despairs, but in you are the treasures of the Kingdom of God! Pull the gem up and let it shine! It is the jewel of JOY!

OF JOY AND JEWELS

"I will greatly rejoice in the LORD; my soul shall exult in my God, for He has clothed me with the garments of salvation; He has covered me with the robe of righteousness, as a bridegroom decks himself like a priest with a beautiful headdress, and as a bride adorns herself with her jewels." Isaiah 61:10

The prophet Daniel referred to Israel as "the Jewel of his kingdom." (Daniel 11:20 NAS) "Israel" includes all of His "heirs of promise."

"And if you are Christ's, then you are Abraham's offspring, heirs according to promise." Galatians 3:29

God's people are His own "treasured possession." They are jewels!

"And they shall be Mine, says the LORD of hosts, in that day when I make up my jewels; and I will spare them, as a man spares his own son that serves him." Malachi 3:17 (KJ2000)

This verse is the basis for the beautiful hymn "When He Cometh." William Orcutt Cushing (1856) wrote it for the children to sing in his Sunday School class.

The last verse goes:

"Little children, little children, who love their Redeemer Are the jewels, precious jewels, His loved and His own."

Here are more of the lyrics:

"When He cometh, when He cometh to make up His jewels, all the jewels, precious jewels, His loved and His own Like the stars of the morning, His bright crown adorning, they shall shine in their beauty. Bright gems for His crown. He will gather, He will gather the gems for His kingdom…."

Yes, the Kingdom of God has many jewels, and they are the believers. The jewels of **JOY** sparkle with their many facets, refracting light, the Light of God.

KINGDOM PARABLES

The LORD Jesus Christ compared the Kingdom of Heaven to precious treasure and encouraged us to seek for it.

In Matthew 13, He spoke to His disciples saying,

"44 The kingdom of heaven is like treasure hidden in a field, which a man found and covered up. Then in his **JOY,** he goes and sells all that he has and buys that field."

In his joy, he goes and sells! The treasure, he will gain is infinitely more precious than "all that he has" on earth!

"45 Again, the kingdom of heaven is like a merchant in search of fine pearls, 46 who, on finding one pearl of great value, went and sold all that he had and bought it.

51 Have you understood all these things?" They said to him, 'Yes.' 52 And he said to them, 'Therefore every scribe who has been trained for the kingdom of heaven is like a master of a house, who brings out of his treasure what is new and what is old.'"

The scribe is aware that the Kingdom principles in the Word are treasures in and of themselves. A disciple of the Word, he's been taught and tutored by the Holy Spirit. A scribe is able to pull up from the Word of God things new and old.

As a new believer, the pastor would preach the Word and my spirit would get so bubbly, I'd want to jump and shout ... but that would've distracted from the teaching. Yet my spirit was jumping on the inside! The "new" word of God was exciting!

Years ago, before my husband was a believer, I was given a dream. My husband and I were pulling out food from a freezer to feed the hungry. This dream was meant to imply that someday we would be feeding the Word of God. These "old" words had seasoned and matured, but they were rock solid as ever. Truth is truth. The "old" words are just as relevant and unchangeable now as ever.

Our LORD Jesus Christ said, "It is the Spirit who gives life; the flesh is no help at all. The words that I have spoken to you are **spirit and life.**" John 6:63

As I sit here and write my spirit rejoices in His Word. The Word of God is a joy!

"I rejoice over Your promise like one who finds vast treasure." Psalm 119:162 (Holman Christian Standard)

"Your words were found, and I ate them, and Your words became to me a **JOY** and the delight of my heart, for I am called by Your name, O LORD, God of hosts." Jeremiah 15:16

THE JOY OF JERUSALEM

The Kingdom is not without a capital, the city of Jerusalem, the city of God's peace. Not so much now in the natural, but He will restore Jerusalem to its former glory and will come to rule and reign over "New" Jerusalem.

Sing and rejoice, O daughter of Zion, for behold, I come and I will dwell in your midst, declares the LORD." Zechariah 2:10

"Beautiful in elevation, is the **JOY** of all the earth, Mount Zion, in the far north, the city of the great King." Psalm 48:2

I had wanted to go to Jerusalem, that city of where my Lord had walked. At that time, I had little hope of going, but I prayed and my prayers were answered rather quickly!

In 1987, I prayed upon hearing about the terror attacks against Jerusalem. I didn't know much about prophecy at that time, but I prayed "Lord, I want to go to Jerusalem before the whole thing is blown up!"

Well, it turns out that within a few days or weeks that my husband came home and said to me that he wanted to go to the "old country." I didn't know quite what he was referring to, but my heart began to beat, and I said, "What old country?" He replied hesitantly because he wasn't yet a believer, "Occupied Jordan." Why I was going to Israel!

My husband had a friend whose roots were around Jericho. His wife, now a citizen, was from Ramallah.

Now, Ramallah had been a Christian town back in the 1950's. My friend told me that it was 100% Christian. The encyclopedia says that it was 95% Christian in 1958. Now, it is almost Muslim in 2015. The Christians had to move out over the years. Many of them are here now in the United States enjoying good lives.

But back in the late eighties, there was still a Christian presence in Ramallah. Sadly, it's almost gone.

But back to my story. I was going to Jerusalem! I had planned on spending ten days there and an additional five days in London. Getting ready for my trip, my husband came and told me that his friend wasn't going. His wife was still going, but he decided not to go, not having the fun of his buddy.

I was devastated. What could I do to persuade him? I spurted out, "I've told all my friends I'm going to Jerusalem!" He ended up saying, "We'll only spend five days in Israel and ten days in London" which was the opposite of our original plans.

So I went along with this proposal, just to see Jerusalem!

Well, it turns out God had different plans.

We arrived in Jordan. The cost of flying there was cheaper. When it was time to go to Israel, we discovered we couldn't. A necessary paper was required to get us in. It was upsetting to me to miss this little important document having once been a travel agent. But somehow I knew the LORD would work this out. He always does. He granted me "the peace that passes all understanding"!

The border agent had told us to pick up the document at the embassy in Amman, which would take us two days. Or we could go over the next day with a tour operator, which happened to be a relative of his. We chose the latter.

Thinking this was to delay our flight, we agreed to change our schedule to a day behind. There weren't any available seats on that day. So we had a "waitlist." (That's when you called the reservationist and put yourself on a "waitlist." Gone are those days!) I was on a waitlist for days. I thought it would come up quickly but it did not. We waited, and waited, and so our days turned into TEN DAYS in Israel and Jordan and five days in London! God got me back to the original plan!

Our entry into Israel began with a one-day Christian tour. David, my husband, wouldn't have chosen a tour like this, complete with Scriptures of what we were seeing. But I was quite happy.

There, in Jerusalem, I introduced my Arabic friends to the "Garden Tomb." Is this the place where Christ could have been buried? Tranquility reigned amid the shrubbery and blossoms. Songs and praises harmonized with prayers and pleas to God. It was so lovely!

My friends, who had lived just twenty minutes outside the city, had never been here. All they had known was the Holy Sepulchre. The "Holy Sepulchre" wasn't holy. It was filled with religious demons. I had attempted to go down to the crypt prior, but my spirit was doing flip-flops! The Holy Spirit did not allow me. Maybe my sensitivities to the religious spirits had something to do with it, but I was definitely getting a decided "NO!" from the Lord.

There are many debates about this, but I believe that the "Garden Tomb" is the place where Christ was buried and, then on the third day, resurrected! It is filled with the peace of the Lord! It is holy ground.

That was my first trip to the Holy Land. It was an answer to prayer. I never realized that I would be back!

"Let my tongue stick to the roof of my mouth, if I do not remember you, if I do not set Jerusalem above my highest JOY!"

Psalm 137:6

JERUSALEM AGAIN

I awoke. It was a dream. Near the end, I had been singing in the spirit over these lush hills. Everyone could hear me singing.

That was many years ago, probably the early 1990's.

Where were those lush hills? I went on many mission trips, but yet I couldn't find them. Then on my fifth trip, in March, 2014, there they were! The lush hills of my dreams.

I had never been to Israel before in the spring time. Never had I seen it in this light, in this view. The land was so plush and the mountains came alive. These hills were so vibrant green! They would not be in a few weeks, the guide told us. Now, I realized why I hadn't seen these lush hills before!

There in the place where years ago the LORD gave His "Sermon on the Mount", I sang. My voice echoed the refrains of glory. It was my dream!

A friend told me that she could hear me singing way up on the hill. In my dream, that was necessary for it was as if everyone heard me singing!

The joy of seeing a dream come to pass! But, we have so much more! We have better delights! We go on to the city of the Lord's praise!

"And this city shall be to me a name of **JOY,** a praise and a glory before all the nations of the earth who shall hear of all the good that I do for them. They shall fear and tremble because of all the good and all the prosperity I provide for it." Jeremiah 33:9

Jerusalem is a joy to behold! Christ walked these hills. Yet we will be going to that eternal city in the sky, the New Jerusalem of God. The old Jerusalem, in this day, is sadly a city of war between the factions of hell and heaven. The New Jerusalem is to be the "City of Peace."

"But be glad and rejoice forever in that which I create; for behold, I create Jerusalem to be a **JOY,** and her people to be a gladness." Isaiah 65:18

The Lord will create the New Jerusalem!

"They shall call you the City of the LORD, the Zion of the Holy One of Israel. Whereas you have been forsaken and hated, with no one passing through, I will make you majestic forever, a **JOY** from age to age." Isaiah 60:14-15

That is City of **JOY** for which we are destined!

ENTER INTO THE JOY OF THE LORD

The parables that Jesus taught in Matthew 24 and 25 are related to the end of the age message that precedes them. This "end of the age" is the context for the Parable of the Talents where we find the master welcoming the faithful servants into "the **JOY** of your master."

14 "For it will be like a man going on a journey, who called his servants and entrusted to them his property. 15 To one he gave five talents, to another two, to another one, to each according to his ability. Then he went away. 16 He who had received the five talents went at once and traded with them, and he made five talents more. 17 So also he who had the two talents made two talents more. 18 But he who had received the one talent went and dug in the ground and hid his master's money. 19 Now after a long time, the master of those servants came and settled accounts with them. 20 And he who had received the five talents came forward, bringing five talents more, saying, 'Master, you delivered to me five talents; here I have made five talents more.' 21 His master said to him, 'Well done, good and faithful servant. You have been faithful over a little; I will set you over much. Enter into the joy of your master.' 22 And he also who had the two talents came forward, saying, 'Master, you delivered to me two talents; here I have made two talents more.' 23 His master said to him, 'Well done, good and faithful servant.

You have been faithful over a little; I will set you over much. Enter into the joy of your master.'" Matthew 25

Those who have been faithful servants of the LORD in this reality will enter into a greater reality and the joy of the LORD! To be in the Presence of the LORD is joy unspeakable! Now we can have a taste of heaven, a taste of His Presence in the spirit realm on earth. But then ….

Perhaps I can best express that inexpressible joy through these my lyrics:

> "Someday I'll see
>
> My King in all His beauty
>
> Someday I'll see
>
> My King enthroned in majesty
>
> Someday I'll see
>
> My wondrous God and King in glory
>
> Someday I'll see.
>
> Oh, glory be! Oh, let it be."

That will be joy unspeakable, joy unfathomable, joy most wonderful, joy sublime!

Here we have an inkling. Here we have a glimmer. Someday we will see Him face to face!

"O Joy of Joys! To now behold My Lord and King! O Joy of Joys! And rhapsody so sweet!"

There is a testimony throughout time, of the joy of the LORD, the joy of being in His Presence:

"You make known to me the path of life; in your Presence there is fullness of **JOY**; at your right hand are pleasures forevermore." Psalm 16:11

Robert Leighton, a 17th-century preacher, expressed his view of the coming heavenly pleasure thusly:

"It is but little that we can receive here, some drops of joy that enter into us; but there we shall enter into **JOY**, as vessels put into a sea of happiness."

THE SEA OF HAPPINESS

Ah, joy in a sea of happiness! What a blissful picture it invokes! Heaven is where God abides and there is a sea of happiness there!

In the heavenly throne room of God, which St. John visited by the spirit, he describes a sea of glass:

"And before the throne, there was as it were a sea of glass, like crystal." Revelation 4:6a

"And I saw what appeared to be a sea of glass mingled with fire—and also those who had conquered the beast and its image and the number of its name, standing beside the sea of glass with harps of God in their hands." Revelation 15:2

Now what John saw was real, real in the spirit realm. He didn't say it was a sea. He said that "it was as it were a sea" and "appeared to be a sea." Had it been a sea, he would have said: "there was a sea." But no, he is describing something he saw that has no identical earthly counterpart. He describes with the best images we will understand.

A real sea is continuously in motion and often even tumultuous. This sea in the heavenly realm is still, calm, at rest as it looks like crystal.

I have seen smaller bodies of water still as glass but never a whole sea! Still waters can best reflect images. When we are still in His Presence we can best reflect God's image. We were created to be a reflection of that holy image.

In this "sea", there are peaceful people. They have no fear of death because they abide in the eternal Life of Christ.

Interestingly, the **new earth** promised in Revelation has no tumultuous sea!

"Then I saw a new heaven and a new earth ... and **the sea was no more**." Revelation 21:1

Perhaps that is saying that there will be no more tumultuous hordes! No more transgressors! No more thieves! No more murderers!

17 "For behold, I create new heavens and a new earth, and the former things shall not be remembered or come into mind. 18 But be glad and rejoice forever in that which I create; for behold, I create Jerusalem to be a **JOY,** and her people to be a gladness. 19 I will rejoice in Jerusalem and be glad in my people; no more shall be heard in it the sound of weeping and the cry of distress. 20 No more shall there be in

it an infant who lives but a few days, or an old man who does not fill out his days, for the young man shall die a hundred years old, and the sinner a hundred years old shall be accursed. 21 They shall build houses and inhabit them; they shall plant vineyards and eat their fruit. 22 They shall not build and another inhabit; they shall not plant and another eat; for like the days of a tree shall the days of my people be, and my chosen shall long enjoy the work of their hands. 23 They shall not labor in vain or bear children for calamity, for they shall be the offspring of the blessed of the LORD, and their descendants with them. 24 Before they call I will answer; while they are yet speaking I will hear. 25 The wolf and the lamb shall graze together; the lion shall eat straw like the ox, and dust shall be the serpent's food. They shall not hurt or destroy in all my holy mountain," says the LORD. Isaiah 65

Wow! That is incredible! I believe I have seen glimpses of this in a few dreams. The animals all have "baby" faces!

A distinction must be made here between the new earth and the throne room of God. The new earth is will be revamped. I cannot say what this will be totally like for this will be a new creation of God.

The throne room has what "appeared to be a sea of glass", which very likely is a "sea" of a tremendous throng, of spirit beings! I base that on Scriptures that equate the Bride of Christ with a city, His holy city Jerusalem, a city of peace!

"'Come, I will show you the Bride, the wife of the Lamb.' And he carried me away in the Spirit to a great, high mountain, and showed me the holy city Jerusalem coming down out of heaven from God" Revelation 21:9b-10

The Bride of Christ is the New Jerusalem for a city is made up of people. It would seem to be that perhaps the New Jerusalem is hovering over the old City. Heaven will be on earth!

"Thy kingdom come. Thy will be done, on earth as it is in heaven." Matthew 6:10 KJ

The critics laugh and scoff at the notion of heaven. They say that Christians believe in pie in the sky. Because they have telescopes that look far into space and yet have not seen God's heaven, they disbelieve. Have they even considered heaven is in a **different dimension**? They mock and disbelieve because they do not want to be accountable to a Creator for their sins!

But we of faith, having our sin problem dealt with through the cross of Christ, know that there is a heavenly eternal state. Yet we can't imagine the glories and joys of heaven fully!

"But, as it is written, 'What no eye has seen, nor ear heard, nor the heart of man imagined, what God has prepared for those who love Him'" 1 Corinthians 2:9

The **JOY** will be marvelous to behold!

THE HEAVENS

"The heavens proclaim the glory of God.
The skies display His craftsmanship."

Psalm 19:1

The word "heaven" in the Bible can mean any one of three heavens depending on the context: the air, outer space, and the third heaven or throne room of God.

The Scriptures say there will be "a new heaven and a new earth."

"Then I saw a new heaven and a new earth, for the first heaven and the first earth had passed away, and the sea was no more." Revelation 21:1

Dr. Jeff Zweerink, an astrophysicist who writes for the ministry *Reasons to Believe,* writes:

"Revelation 20–21 and other biblical descriptions of the forthcoming creation imply a new physical realm with some new physics not at work in the current universe.

For example, New Jerusalem is described as a cube measuring 12,000 stadia (about 1,400 miles) on each side. Such a structure cannot exist in the present universe because gravity would force something that size into a sphere. Thus, it appears that the new creation must exhibit some different form of gravity." [3]

That's an interesting thought! I'm not sure it's a cube, maybe it's more like a pyramid or mountain with a base of 1400 x 1400 miles (foursquare) and reaching to a height of 1400 miles. But it'll be spectacular!

God's highest heaven, the third heaven, His Mount Zion with its New Jerusalem is coming to earth! It will be like a sun to the new earth, providing its light.

"I did not see a temple in the city, because the Lord God Almighty and the Lamb are its temple. The city does not need the sun or the moon to shine on it, for the glory of God gives it light, and the Lamb is its lamp. The nations will walk by its light, and the kings of the earth will bring their splendor into it." Revelation 21:22-24

"The sun shall be no more your light by day, nor for brightness shall the moon give you light; but the LORD will be your everlasting light, and your God will be your glory." Isaiah 60:19

From these and other Scriptures, we know:

* The LORD dwells in the New Jerusalem.

* The glory of the LORD is the light to the city and to the new earth.

---

[3] *http://www.reasons.org/articles/q-a-does-the-book-of-revelation-hint-at-a-multiverse*

* The LORD's Bride, the holy saints of God populate this city.
* The city is made of pure gold!
* There are still nations on the new earth.

Sounds glorious whether you take these verses metaphorically, literally, or both! I take them both ways! So the streets may be of golden hue but the saints there are of pure gold quality, having all been perfected in Christ! But here's the clincher:

"Nothing impure will ever enter it, nor will anyone who does what is shameful or deceitful, but only those whose names are written in the Lamb's book of life." Revelation 21:27

"Nothing impure" within this city assures the joy and tranquility of the home of the saints. The New Jerusalem from which the saints rule with Christ as their head is a perfect place! It is better than the Garden of Paradise! It is the best because the LORD of all the universe dwells there!

"For You make him most blessed forever; You make him glad with the JOY of your Presence."
Psalm 21:6

ENTRY DENIED

"…but only those whose names are written in the Lamb's book of life" will abide there in the Jerusalem of gold! Indeed, the unrighteous will not be allowed entry!

There are other Scriptures that make the same declaration:

"But as for the cowardly, the faithless, the detestable, as for murderers, the sexually immoral, sorcerers, idolaters, and all liars, their portion will be in the lake that burns with fire and sulfur, which is the second death." Revelation 21:8

"Outside are the dogs and sorcerers and the sexually immoral and murderers and idolaters, and everyone who loves and practices falsehood." Revelation 22:15

"Or do you not know that the unrighteous will not inherit the kingdom of God? Do not be deceived: neither the sexually immoral, nor idolaters, nor adulterers, nor men who practice homosexuality, nor thieves, nor the greedy, nor drunkards, nor revilers, nor swindlers will inherit the kingdom of God." 1 Corinthians 6:9-10

Jesus answered, "Truly, truly, I say to you, unless one is born of water and the Spirit, he cannot enter the kingdom of God." John 3:5

"Unfair!" cries the unrighteous! God is King! He has a perfect Kingdom and if you want entry, you must come through Christ.

"I am the way, and the truth, and the life. No one comes to the Father except through Me." (John 14:6)

If you want to be politically correct, don't ever preach on hell. If you want to be right with God and if you want God's best for people, speak the truth in love. Love would not withhold the Truth, the only way into abundant life and **JOY!**

THE FACADE OF SATAN

God blesses and offers abundant life to His people, those who receive Him as LORD and Redeemer. He offers them eternal life in His glorious Presence!

What does the dark kingdom offer? They have nothing good to offer, only lies and counterfeits! The enemy of our soul, Satan, and his minions entice with counterfeits of true joy.

God is and speaks truth. Satan offers lies and deception and illusions of happiness.

God is and beams light. The enemy can appear as an angel of light, but it is artificial and false.

God is love and freely gives love. The enemy offers lust.

God offers inner joy. The enemy offers momentary indulgence.

The dark side offers transient pleasure. Evil entices with pleasures in revelries, pleasures in drunkenness and highs, pleasures in forbidden fruit, pleasures in altered states, and pleasures of sin. And it's all a facade. Sooner or later the truth is revealed and the momentary pleasure yields the fruit of ill health and death.

Sinners find pleasure in bawdiness, perversion, and revelry. At worst, some find pleasure in death and destruction. But their pleasure is short-lived. Soon the law catches up with them. And if the law doesn't catch up with them, Judgment Day looms. We all must face our Maker.

But the consequences of sin follow the short-lived rowdiness and partying:

"And the Lord struck the people with a plague because of what they did with the calf Aaron had made." Exodus 32:35

Haman, the evil enemy of the Jews, rejoiced briefly:

"And Haman went out that day joyful and glad of heart." Esther 5:9

But justice prevailed in the end:

"And the king said, 'Hang him on that.' So they hanged Haman on the gallows that he had prepared for Mordecai. Then the wrath of the king abated." Esther 7:10

"Do not be deceived: God is not mocked, for whatever one sows, that will he also reap." Galatians 6:7

Being seduced by momentary sinful pleasures compared to eternal glories and joys is plain foolishness! Repent, and turn to God for deliverance! Just cry out, "Save me, Jesus Christ!"

St. Peter declared,

"Let it be known to all of you and to all the people of Israel that by the name of Jesus Christ of Nazareth, whom you crucified, whom God raised from the dead ... there is salvation in no one else, for there is no other name under heaven given among men by which we must be saved." Acts 4:10,12

"And it shall come to pass that everyone who calls on the name of the LORD shall be saved." Joel 2:32a

*"May we shout for **JOY** over your salvation ..."*

Psalm 20:5a

EVERLASTING JOY

*"And the ransomed of the LORD shall return and come to Zion with singing; everlasting **JOY** shall be upon their heads; they shall obtain **gladness and joy**, and sorrow and sighing shall flee away."* Isaiah 35:10

So the righteous will escape from the wrath of God and enter into the spiritual Mount Zion and the New Jerusalem! Heaven will be joined with earth! And the prayer that we all have been praying for centuries will come about:

"Thy kingdom come. Thy will be done in earth, as it is in heaven." Matthew 6:10 KJ

The Kingdom of God on earth! And the saints to be the kings and priests!

"And hath made us kings and priests unto God and his Father; to Him be glory and dominion for ever and ever. Amen." Revelation 1:6

"The one who conquers and who keeps my works until the end, to him I will give authority over the nations …" Revelation 2:26

"'But the saints of the Most High shall receive the kingdom and possess the kingdom forever, forever and ever.'" Daniel 7:18

And so the meek "shall inherit the earth." HalleluYAH! This is the glorious promise to the redeemed of the LORD! Everlasting **JOY!**

THE SONG OF JOY

MUSIC, MUSIC

"Sing aloud to God our strength;
*shout for **JOY** to the God of Jacob!"* Psalm 81:1

Maybe we just don't sing enough. Maybe what we sing is negative. The standing joke for country western music is that you lose your job, you lose your girl, you lose your dog, and you lose your truck. How are you going to get built up listening to those lyrics? The words we mouth or sing affect us.

Music is a precious gift. God created it and did so splendidly. It can be perverted and misused to manipulate emotions and to bring out the worst in human nature. OR it can elevate one to spiritual heights of rhapsody. Combined with the words of Scripture, it is a powerful weapon and tool for life.

Maybe your church doesn't do much congregational singing. Maybe they have "professionals." But everybody needs to sing! After all, we were created for praise!

"The people whom I formed for Myself that they might declare My praise." Isaiah 43:21

There is a local highway ad to bring you from "road rage" to "road praise"! A local Christian Houston radio channel sponsors it. A little praise and worship to God Almighty will get your day off to a positive start!

THE SONG OF JOY

The Redeemed of the LORD have a marvelous hope. We can access the joy, the joy of the Spirit, now!

"But be filled with the Spirit, addressing one another in psalms and hymns and spiritual songs, singing and making melody to the Lord with your heart" Ephesians 5:18-19

"Let the word of Christ dwell in you richly, teaching and admonishing one another in all wisdom, singing psalms and hymns and spiritual songs, with **thankfulness** in your hearts to God." Colossians 3:16

Singing songs of joy is a simple way to access the Kingdom joy inside. Admittedly, I may have a slight advantage here in that I was created to be a songbird. But a lack of talent shouldn't stop anyone from singing their praise to God, but pride might.

Sometimes we musically gifted ones can be a bit snobbish. A former pastor, who himself was gifted vocally, told us this story. He became annoyed listening to a lady squeak out a song. The LORD rebuked him, telling him that He enjoys her singing! Perhaps all our singing is filtered as it goes up to heaven! So make a joyful noise!

*"Make a **JOYFUL** noise to the LORD, all the earth; break forth into **JOYOUS** song and sing praises!"*

Psalm 98:4

SHAKING OFF THE SPIRIT OF HEAVINESS

"Sing and rejoice, O daughter of Zion!"
Zechariah 2:10

Spiritual songs scare off the spirit of heaviness. The wisdom of the Scripture reveals praise to God. The LORD dwells in the praises of His people. So put on "the garment of praise for the spirit of heaviness"! Isaiah 61:3 (KJ)

Focusing on God will be a source of joy. The Scriptures, even if not sung, act as an antidote for gloom.

There is a children's song with the Scripture verse:

"The joy of the LORD is my strength…" Nehemiah 8:10

If you sing happy Scripture songs, it'll draw that joy right up and out from within you.

"Therefore, with **JOY** shall ye draw water out of the wells of salvation." Isaiah 12:3

How does one draw up that living water of joy? One could sing the praise of our Savior's blessings!

"If you want joy you must sing for it … shout for it … jump for it!"

While you don't have to work for the gift of joy, singing and dancing unto the LORD are great ways, maybe the easiest ways, to access that joy deep inside you.

"For this reason, I remind you to fan into flame the gift of God, which is in you …" 2 Timothy 1:6

Don't be too prideful to sing simple **JOYOUS** children's songs because "to such belongs the kingdom of heaven." Matthew 19:14

LEAPING TO PRAISE THE LORD

"So let's all positively leap up, leap up, leap up and keep on praising!"

(From the Granny Vee CD "Positive Praise!")

I've slowed down from this lately, not being physically able to leap too well in my senior years. But for many years, Granny Vee, my alter ego, would go on mission trips and visit orphanages with my puppet Friendly Phil the Frog. It is an absolute joy to lead children in praise to God! Children can be so exuberant in their praise!

Jesus said, "Truly, I say to you, whoever does not receive the kingdom of God like a child shall not enter it." (Luke 18:17)

We can enter into the joy of that Kingdom by following the example of children in jubilant praise as well!

Here are some examples of what we sang together:

"Praise Him with a thumping beat

Praise Him as you stomp your feet

Praise Him as you twirl around
Praise Him with a joyful sound!"
(Shout "HALLELUYAH!")

(From "Listen, Children" on the Granny Vee CD "Positive Praise!")

That is based on Psalm 150:

1 Praise the LORD!
Praise God in His sanctuary;
praise Him in His mighty heavens!
2 Praise Him for His mighty deeds;
praise Him according to His excellent greatness!
3 Praise Him with trumpet sound;
praise Him with lute and harp!
4 Praise Him with tambourine and dance;
praise Him with strings and pipe!
5 Praise Him with sounding cymbals;
praise Him with loud clashing cymbals!
6 Let everything that has breath praise the LORD!
Praise the LORD!

Here's a song about keeping a positive outlook!

POSITIVE PRAISE

"I'm sitting on a positive pad
Don't want to dwell on things that are sad
I'm keepin' my sight on things high
'Cause how can I leap up if I don't even try?
I'm sitting on a positive pad
You can be, too: just smile and be glad!
'Cause it's a beautiful day
So what if the sky is gray!
I'm leaping along
With this cheery, little song:
La, la, la, la, la
La, la, la, la, la, la, la!
La, la, la, la, la
La, la, la, la, la, la, la!"

(From "Positive Pad" on the Granny Vee CD "Happity Birthday!")

I love the "La-la" chorus. It is reminiscent of the "Lai-lai-lai" refrains in happy Jewish melodies. I've been told they sing that as the King enters! King Jesus Christ certainly will come again. Get ready for His **JOYOUS** return!

SILENCING THE SONGBIRD

From early on, the devil tried to keep me from my destiny as a psalmist. Perhaps he follows the anointing in family lines and tries to destroy the good seeds before they ever have a chance to grow.

My mother had a beautiful voice. Back then, before the big conglomerates of media, local talent could get on the airwaves. My mother played guitar and sang country western on the radio in New Jersey. She taught me to yodel. She groomed me for my first solo at my kindergarten graduation, singing "Somewhere Over the Rainbow."

But then my mother died, leaving my dad with five children. My song died. I sang somewhat at church in the children's choir but my mother, my mentor was gone. I think now, that perhaps I should have joined the Glee Club in high school, but I wasn't really aware of it. I had no one guiding me, raising me up in the way I should go, which I understand in the Hebrew also includes directing a child along their chosen path. I don't recall much music in our home after my mother died. No one encouraged me to sing. For over twenty years my vocal talent lay dormant.

In my teens, I strayed away from the LORD. Then I naively joined a quasi-New Age Buddhist cult because it touted itself as a philosophy, not a religion. It promised world peace. I moved to Texas and got married to someone else in the cult. Some years later, a neighbor was witnessing to me about the LORD. After her whole church, Evangelistic Temple in Houston, brought my name before the LORD in prayer, I was delivered.

Jesus Christ visited me in the Spirit and downloaded truths into my being. I awoke with the lingering vision of His face. My life has never been the same again. [4]

The music, the worship at Evangelistic Temple was incredible. The Spirit of the LORD was strong there in those days. I joined the choir. When I first heard the song "I've Just Seen Jesus" tears welled up in me. It was so my testimony! I just had to sing that song! I asked the music minister. In reality, I was not quite ready for prime time, but he recognized my gift. So he gave me a short solo. Bless his heart! He could see that I was nervous when I got up to sing. My whole leg was shaking. So he kindly asked me a few questions about how I had come to Jesus to start me off.

And that's how I came to be singing for the LORD. And ever since then, I've sung that song "I've Just Seen Jesus", personalizing some of the lyrics to fit my testimony.

So the devil had thought that he had silenced this songbird, but no! It may be that the LORD used the devil to keep me from going into popular music which nowadays

---

[4] *A more detailed account of how Christ delivered me may be found on my website:* https://hisinheritance.org/about-2/

can be a real rat race, and worst. I have the greatest honor to sing for and before the King of Kings!

One of those early days at Evangelistic Temple, I turned to a close friend in the choir, with this observation: "Did you know that a lot of these songs we're singing are in the Bible?" She laughed.

And that is the key. Singing Scripture-based songs is a great way to get the Word into your heart and to remember them. God's word doesn't return void and empty! So singing Scripture songs strengthened me! I sang of His love when I felt unloved. I sang of His strength when I was weak. I sang throughout the day and it kept the "spirit of heaviness" at bay. My LORD was my joy and I expressed it joyfully in song!

That singing played an invaluable part in enabling me to persist in prayer for twenty years for my husband's salvation! The songs lifted my spirit when perhaps otherwise I might have despaired. Singing was my strength.

*"Sing for **JOY** to God our strength; shout aloud to the God of Jacob!"*

Psalm 81:1

A TIME TO WEEP

"Rejoice with those who rejoice, weep with those who weep."
Romans 12:15

Well, let's face it - sometimes we just don't feel like singing or dancing! And sometimes singing or dancing is not even appropriate.

"For everything, there is a season, and a time for every matter under heaven ... a time to weep, and a time to laugh; a time to mourn, and a time to dance; There is a time for grief" Ecclesiastes 3:1,4

There is a time to grieve, a time to mourn, a time to be sad. Jesus wept. The Holy Spirit is grieved. Those are emotions that we all share. But they are for a season, not a lifetime of dreariness.

Women have a tendency to live by their emotions. "I don't feel like it." But the Word admonishes us to walk in the Spirit! Our emotions should be submitted to the Holy Spirit. The Spirit in us can grieve, but it also rejoices.

The psalmist David, under the inspiration of the Holy Spirit, goes from despair to confidence and hope in the LORD all in a matter of a few verses! He goes from "weary with my moaning" to "the LORD has heard the sound of my moaning."

6 I am weary with my moaning; every night I flood my bed with tears; I drench my couch with my weeping. 7 My eye wastes away because of grief; it grows weak because of

all my foes. 8 Depart from me, all you workers of evil, for the LORD has heard the sound of my weeping. 9 The LORD has heard my plea; the LORD accepts my prayer. 10 All my enemies shall be ashamed and greatly troubled; they shall turn back and be put to shame in a moment. Psalm 6

Have you been weary with moaning? Have you flooded your bed with tears? I have, too! But when we bring those things to the LORD, He comforts us and gives us hope. Here we see the psalmist express that glorious transformation in one verse:

"When anxiety was great within me, Your consolation brought me joy." Psalm 94:19

"Cast your burden on the LORD, and He will sustain you; He will never permit the righteous to be moved." Psalm 55:22

Whatever is happening in your life, cast your burden on the LORD and rejoice because God is in control and loves you!

When we were a young married couple, we ended up in financial difficulties through some bad choices and some bad circumstances, namely a fire. The LORD told me when I prayed about it, not to worry about it! What? Don't worry about unpaid bills? We continued to make payments on them, but I tried to quit worrying about them. It turns out that our financial mess, which got worse before better, might have been a significant factor in bringing my husband to the LORD! Sometimes we just have to go through things. Truly, the LORD is always working it out for my ultimate **JOY!**

FOR YOUR GOOD

"And we know that for those who love God all things work together for good, for those who are called according to his purpose." Romans 8:28

Whatever is happening in your life, God has a promise to His saints. "All things work together" for good for me! Now there's something to rejoice about!

There are two conditions for that amazing promise. Do you love God? I certainly do!

The other is that this promise is for "those who are called according to His purpose." Now it stands to reason that if the LORD saved you and caused you to be born again of His Spirit, and placed His Spirit in you, then you must be "called according to His purpose."

For some reason, maybe due to fleshly yearnings, one may not be walking in His purposes now. Oh, but He'll get one there unless one is too stubborn! Certain things may lead one to that point! Until they do, it may be a sorry set of circumstances that lead you back to the LORD! But that's for our good!

When my husband's business failed, it worked to bring him to His Savior! That's a day to remember!

The enemy sold Joseph into slavery. For a while, he was kept locked up in a cell. But when he was released, he was there to spare his family the hardships of a drought. The devil "meant evil against me, but God meant it for good…" Genesis 50:20

If you are a believer, whatever is happening in your life, of this you may be confident: God will make it work together for your good and your eventual **JOY!**

GREATER IS HE THAT IS IN ME

"Little children, you are from God and have overcome them, for He who is in you is greater than he who is in the world."

1 John 4:4

The Buddhists have a curse. They warned us that if we were to get rid of our idolatrous scroll housed in an altar in our homes, we would die in like manner. They told stories such as a man throwing this scroll in the lake and then later himself drowning. Now, I can see how manipulative those stories were! But back then we were somewhat brainwashed through the monotonous chanting and propaganda.

After I had been delivered, the LORD instructed me to get rid of this scroll. This would not go well with my husband, I was sure. I asked the LORD to confirm His Word. As a new believer, not knowing the Word well, I opened my Bible and read a verse about throwing out idols. Three times I opened my Bible and read a similar verse.

"And a number of those who had practiced magic arts brought their books together and burned them in the sight of all. And they counted the value of them and found it came to fifty thousand pieces of silver." Acts 19:19

Many Christians do not realize that idols and wicked things give the enemy an open door to wreak havoc on their lives. We need to clean our homes of things displeasing to the LORD, including some religious souvenirs we've picked up along the way. I know this now, but back then, it was because the LORD pointed it out to me.

Now, one of those Scripture-based songs I had been singing came in really handy. The Buddhists had a curse, but I knew "Greater is He that is in me, than He that is in the world!" I gave no worry to their curse but declared God's Word.

So I burnt up my husband's scroll and threw out the altar with the trash. Knowing he'd be livid, I took the kids and moved in with his mom for a few days till he calmed down.

But afterward, when we went back home, my toddler son came to me saying, "Mommy, the houseman is gone."

"What houseman?" I asked as goosebumps went up my arms.

My little David had seen a demon! I had never talked to my son about such things. Where would he get this idea, if not true? No wonder we had been having such confrontations. A "familiar spirit" had been hanging around to stir up strife! The idol in our home gave the demon legal access, but now it was gone! I thanked God for His instruction to throw out the cursed things. Our Father knows best! I filled my home with worship and song. Our family life took a smoother course.

So not only did I burn up the idolatrous scroll in our home, but I boldly convinced a few friends to allow me to burn their scrolls up as well. The devil was mad! And I had a **JOYOUS** victory!

THROUGH FLOOD AND FIRE

1 But now thus says the LORD,

He who created you, O Jacob,

He who formed you, O Israel:

"Fear not, for I have redeemed you;

I have called you by name, you are mine.

2 When you pass through the waters, I will be with you;

and through the rivers, they shall not overwhelm you;

when you walk through fire you shall not be burned,

and the flame shall not consume you.

Isaiah 43

The devil had an assignment out on me. Old slew foot wanted me dead by flames. Well, the devil tried, but my Daddy is bigger!

"Fire! Get out!" my husband yelled. I grabbed our baby daughter and ran out to watch our new home burn.

Had the devil won a round? Hardly! God does work all things for my good! And I held on to that promise as I watched the fire consume our roof.

We had bought a new home in Jersey Village, a small community that made me think of my New Jersey roots. I was so appreciative to the LORD for this new home! Our family had grown and we needed more space. We had two boys and now the baby girl, herself an answer to very specific prayer!

But Christmas was not to be spent in our new home. For the first time since we had been married, we went out of town for Christmas, spending it with family in Dallas. When we returned home, we noticed that our home had been flooded. The carpet was soaked through.

Many a folk in Houston might remember the winter freeze of December 1989. It was rumored that up to one-third the homes in Houston had their pipes freeze overnight. That's an unusual phenomenon for Houston. The homes had been built without thought to protecting pipes. That has changed since then!

Anyway, because we had been away and because of the great demand, it took us three weeks to get a plumber over to fix the broken pipes. It seems now that somehow a ground wire had been attached to one of the pulled pipes, for three days after the broken pipes were replaced, we had a fire which started on the wall in the kitchen.

They say God works in mysterious ways. The night before the fire, I took our baby into bed with me. She had a fever and would be tossing and turning all night. I suggested to my husband that he might sleep better on the couch, considering Natalie would be restless.

Had not our baby been sick, things might have been worse. But since she was ill, Dad was on the couch. Since Dad was on the couch that night, being closer to the kitchen, he awoke in time to get us all out of danger.

We had recently installed a fire alarm, but it was not working due to the flood we had just experienced. Natalie being sick and Dad on the couch were blessings in disguise! God was watching over us!

As I stood outside, I watched as the flames leaped over the shackle roof. Strangely, I was not upset. I was thankful all my family was alive! And I was holding on to the promise of God. He would work this out for my good. How I did not know! But He gave me peace.

That year 1990 was not a cake-walk. It was probably the hardest year of my life. I had three small children and was homeless. Raising three children is demanding even with a stable home. We were far from stable for a year.

But at least we had some place to stay. At first, we were at a hotel. A neighbor graciously allowed me to do my laundry at her home. When the insurance money ran out for temporary housing, we moved back into our former home which we had rented out. Another blessing in disguise was that the renters were not paying so we evicted them and moved in ourselves. But then my husband's secretary needed a place to live, so we rented it to her, knowing we would have a good tenant for years to come.

So I went on a summer vacation with my kids. We stayed a while with my sister in upstate New York. But on return, I was supposed to be staying at my husband's client's beach home but we couldn't get in. I had been on the road with three small kids for too long and broke down and cried in frustration. Where was my song? My quiet time with the LORD, a source of strength, had disappeared. I had very little time alone at all.

A friend from church, hearing my plight, invited me to stay with her for a while. She was a single-parent mom with kids around the same age as my children. It was a good arrangement for both of us for a few months. We became good friends over that time. We have stayed friends all these years, another **JOY** and a blessing!

JOY IN THE VICTORY

So how did God work all this out for my good? The biggest blessing was obviously we were alive and well! We had not a burn from the fire meant to kill!

The second blessing was my husband's ties to the Buddhists were cut! Cults have a way of holding onto people. They keep one so busy with activities and duties that you haven't much time for even family. My husband is an attorney which is demanding enough without having to go to Buddhist meetings all the time. He was spending more time with them than with us. The boys needed him.

The fire gave my husband an excuse to break with the Buddhist rigid schedules. He poured his energy into tearing down the burnt house himself, saving the money to build a second story onto it. Since he was so preoccupied, he stopped going to Buddhist meetings. Now he had more time with me and his children and did not miss out on their growing years. What a blessing! What an answer to my prayer!

The Buddhists had wanted him to go on a pilgrimage overseas. I didn't want him to go. Had he gone, he would be absent at the time of the fire. Thinking about this, I brought it to his attention, a little later. Had he gone overseas, he might have come home to no house, no wife, no children. Had he done what the Buddhists wanted, he could've ended up losing everything! We, on the other hand, would've gone to be with the LORD in eternity!

We were eating one day at a Chinese restaurant. The waitress was one of the Buddhists. She told me had I not stopped chanting, there might not have been a fire, implying that the chanting would've protected me. I told her that God had protected me and my family from death and for that I was grateful. Interestingly, her own home burnt down some time later. I guess chanting is not fire-insurance, after all!

What the devil meant for evil, God turned around and used for my good. We were all alive. I had more time with my husband. The children had more of their dad. He was free of the cult. And we had a bigger home with almost everything new!

The devil lost. My husband was no longer in his clutch. Thank you, LORD! I went through a flood, a fire, and a stressful year but I came out with a victory for my family! Hallelujah! Thank you, Jesus Christ! There is great **JOY** in such victory!

COUNT IT ALL JOY

Even though that was a tough year, by the grace of God, I endured. I should have been counting each day, each trial as "all joy." But as a babe in Christ, I was still not aware.

It was a testing of my faith in His promise. I endured holding onto His promise that He would work all this out. What I didn't know was that He was also working steadfastness in me!

"Count it all joy, my brothers, when you meet trials of various kinds, for you know that the testing of your faith produces steadfastness. And let steadfastness have its full effect, that you may be perfect and complete, lacking in nothing." James 1:2-4

That steadfastness will perfect my character and one day I hope to hear these words:

"Well done, good and faithful servant; you were faithful over a few things, I will make you ruler over many things. Enter into the joy of your Lord." Matthew 25:21

By the grace of God, I remained faithful to pray for my husband. Through tempestuous times, through flood and fire, through ordeals, my LORD wanted me to endure in prayer for my husband. That was His will. After, over twenty years of prayer for him, my husband prayed to receive Christ and has been growing ever since. That is my eternal joy. It is also a joy to the LORD, for it was not His will for my husband to perish.

If your spouse doesn't yet know the LORD, believe me, it's hard. But the reward is great! Your love and prayers will one day be answered. Your tears and persistence in prayer will be turned into amazing joy!

Maybe you are enduring through another kind of ordeal. Whatever it is, remain faithful, counting it "all joy" because great is your reward in heaven!

Your faithfulness and obedient labor will yield the fruit of joy and you will hear the words spoken from our Savior's lips: "Well done! Enter into the joy of your LORD!"

But you protest, "I can't 'count it all joy!'" Well, yes, you can, if you will walk by faith and not by sight! If you walk in the Spirit, and not by your feelings! If you make a decision to walk according to the Word of God. That is where it begins. A decision! Once your will (part of your soul) decides to do things God's way, His grace will help change you. Is this not how your new life in Christ began? You made a decision with your will to accept Jesus Christ as your LORD and Savior?

"Are you so foolish? Having begun by the Spirit, are you now being perfected by the flesh? …. So then, those who are of faith are blessed along with Abraham, the man of faith." Galatians 3:3,9

Walk as men of faith, confident that God will work all things for one's **JOY** and one's good!

THE
BEATITUDES

THE BEATITUDES

Blessed are the poor in spirit, for theirs is
the kingdom of heaven.

Blessed are those who mourn,
for they shall be comforted.

Blessed are the meek,
for they shall inherit the earth.

Blessed are those who hunger and thirst for righteousness,
for they shall be satisfied.

Blessed are the merciful,
for they shall receive mercy.

Blessed are the pure in heart,

for they shall see God.

Blessed are the peacemakers,
for they shall be called sons of God.

Blessed are those who are persecuted
for righteousness' sake,
for theirs is the kingdom of heaven.

Blessed are you when others revile you and persecute you and utter all kinds of evil against you falsely on my account. Rejoice and be glad, for your reward is great in heaven ..."
Matthew 5:3-12

NOTE: Granny Vee, the author's alias, has also written lessons for children on the Beatitudes on grannyvee.com under the Proverbs tab.

JOYFUL ARE THE BLESSED!

We truly are blessed to be delivered "from the domain of darkness and transferred" into "the kingdom of His beloved Son." Colossians 1:13

We truly are blessed because He has "blessed us in Christ with every spiritual blessing in the heavenly places." Ephesians 1:3

And we truly are blessed in that Christ taught us how to be a blessing!

Jesus Christ instructed us in the Beatitudes how to come to Him and live as He would Himself being a blessing Young's Literal Translation uses the word "happy" instead of "blessed" which indeed is an appropriate aspect of the Greek word. Matthew Henry in his time-honored Commentary explains:

"The poor in spirit are happy.... Those that mourn are happy.... The meek are happy.... Heaven is the joy of our Lord; a mountain of joy..."

Therefore, to be blessed is to have spiritual happiness, spiritual joy! So Jesus Himself was teaching a great lesson on true **JOY** in the Sermon on the Mount!

The old Hollywood portrayals of Christ as sober and serious might lead some to think Jesus was teaching on how to be sanctimoniously religious. But it was not the LORD's intent for His followers to be down-in-the-mouth doormats. He was teaching us to live in the Spirit realm, above the dreary condition of the wretched! His teachings are above this world! His teachings are full of **JOY!**

THE BEATITUDES
EIGHT CHARACTERISTICS OF JOYFUL FOLK

HAPPY ARE THE POOR IN SPIRIT

If you want to be happy, be poor in spirit. The word comes from a Greek word that means "to crouch or cower like a beggar." Isaiah was a man who "crouched like a beggar", so-to-speak when he heard voice of the LORD:

"And I said: 'Woe is me! For I am lost; for I am a man of unclean lips, and I dwell in the midst of a people of unclean lips; for my eyes have seen the King, the LORD of hosts!' Then one of the seraphim flew to me, having in his hand a burning coal that he had taken with tongs from the altar. And he touched my mouth and said: 'Behold, this has touched your lips; your guilt is taken away, and your sin atoned for.' And I heard the voice of the Lord saying, 'Whom shall I send, and who will go for us?' Then I said, 'Here I am! Send me.'" Isaiah 6:5-8

When Jesus Christ met the centurion, the LORD replied to him that He would come to heal his servant.

"But the centurion replied, 'Lord, I am not worthy to have you come under my roof, but only say the word, and my servant will be healed.'" Matthew 8:8

Not only was the centurion one of great faith, but his humility is clear. He was poor in spirit. Happy are those who ask of God for circumstances beyond their control!

Happy are those who know they need God.

Happy are those who are aware of assistance from His Spirit.

Happy are they that acknowledge you need a Savior!

They are happy to know that the LORD will pour into them spiritual riches to overflowing! They then become a channel through which His Spirit constantly emanates!

"And I will be like a stream of your living water that extends your love to the world" (my lyrics)

Now how happy is that?

… BUT UNHAPPY ARE THE ARROGANT

Now, let's look at the opposite of being "poor in spirit." How many arrogant and proud people could be classified as joyful people? How many hardened atheists are truly joyful?

"They pour out their arrogant words; all the evildoers boast." Psalm 94:4

Says the LORD: "I will punish the world for its evil, and the wicked for their iniquity; I will put an end to the pomp of the arrogant, and lay low the pompous pride of the ruthless." Isaiah 13:11

"'Scoffer' is the name of the arrogant, haughty man who acts with arrogant pride." Proverbs 21:24

"Pride goes before destruction, and a haughty spirit before a fall." Proverbs 16:18

We know that verse! But what about the following:

"It is better to be of a **lowly spirit with the poor** than to divide the spoil with the proud." Proverbs 16:19

A lowly spirit is indeed happy! The humble have **JOY** as their reward, both here and now and in the next!

HAPPY ARE THEY THAT MOURN

If you want to be happy, mourn. Ah, this does seem like an oxymoron, but such can be the Kingdom of God! But here is how that works. God turns our mourning around!

"Then shall the young women rejoice in the dance, and the young men and the old shall be merry. I will turn their mourning into **JOY**; I will comfort them, and give them gladness for sorrow." Jeremiah 31:13

"Rejoice with Jerusalem, and be glad for her, all you who love her; **rejoice with her in joy**, all you who mourn over her" Isaiah 66:10

Mourning is turned into joy. Whoever spends much time in prayer to the LORD, is happiest when that petition is answered.

Hannah said, "I am a woman troubled in spirit." (1 Samuel 1:15) Her answer came in the little baby Samuel.

Samuel was to be a mighty prophet and that gave Hannah great joy!

... BUT UNHAPPY ARE THEY THAT COULDN'T CARE LESS

Perhaps the unhappy are seen in the church of Laodicea. Do they seem to be a people who mourn? Would they petition the LORD with all their souls? A passionate people, they are not. They are lukewarm. Lukewarm people don't cry out to heaven!

"'I know your works: you are neither cold nor hot. Would that you were either cold or hot! So, because you are lukewarm, and neither hot nor cold, I will spit you out of my mouth." Revelation 3:15-16

They see themselves as rich. They know nothing of the sorrow that takes place around them. They have it all! But they don't see what they are missing. They don't know how to mourn over the Church at large: the saints being tested, the saints being persecuted, and the saints being martyred.

"For you say, I am rich, I have prospered, and I need nothing, not realizing that you are wretched, pitiable, poor, blind, and naked. I counsel you to buy from me gold refined by fire, so that you may be rich, and white garments so that you may clothe yourself and the shame of your nakedness may not be seen, and salve to anoint your eyes, so that you may see. Those whom I love, I reprove and discipline, so be zealous and repent." Revelation 3:17-19

Would the church at Laodicea mourn! That would undo the lukewarmness. Perhaps they were not a church who prayed, except for their own selfish reasons.

The churches, when I was younger, were always praying, here in my neck of the woods. They had Wednesday night prayer meetings. The churches now are full of entertainment and basketball and luncheons and parties, but have they forgotten prayer? There's nothing wrong in all this fancy extravagance, and some of them may be used to bring the lost, but where is prayer?

Happy are those who still pray! My church does. And prayer meetings are organized by many para-church ministries. May they be blessed!

Jesus Christ said:

"Truly, truly, I say to you, you will weep and lament, but the world will rejoice. You will be sorrowful, but your sorrow will turn into JOY."

John 16:20

HAPPY ARE THE MEEK

It is not the proud self-willed people who will inhabit the Kingdom of God. It is those who are submitted to the Almighty.

Meekness is not weakness. Meekness is strength of character coupled with self-control. It is humility to obey our Creator.

"Seek the LORD, all you humble of the land, who do His just commands; seek righteousness; seek humility; perhaps you may be hidden on the day of the anger of the LORD." Zephaniah 2:3

The prophet Zephaniah reveals how to be hidden through judgment. Indeed, the very name "Zephaniah" means "the LORD hides." That's very comforting in times of disaster. Wouldn't you be grateful if you were hidden through disasters?

But the LORD will restore the meek to the land.

"He shall scorn the scorners, and to the meek He will give grace." Proverbs 3:34 DRB

This is the theme of Psalm 37: the wicked will be no more and the meek shall inherit the land.

"But the meek shall inherit the land and delight themselves in abundant peace." Psalm 37:11

... BUT UNHAPPY ARE THE CONTROL-FREAKS

Now look at the opposite. How many control-freaks are truly joyous? When everything is dandy, it's fine. But they fly off the handle when someone upsets their order, even God.

"As long as everything is exactly the way I want it, I'm totally flexible." (*Gilmore Girls* quote by Amy Sherman-Palladino)

This is a popular idiom so it's easy to label individuals as control-freaks. Some people may have an "excellent spirit" (Daniel 6:3), but it could be *perceived* as a control-freak by a shiftless loafer.

Control-freaks strive to dictate. The "strife, jealousy, fits of anger", all works of the flesh, (Galatians 5:20) could be transfigured into virtue. They could be transformed to the Spirit-led qualities of gentleness and meekness, with a change of heart. That's the work of the Holy Ghost: to reroute those personality disorders into something constructive. So if one has a little control-freak in them, the LORD is able to transform. It could bloom into a sweet-tempered "excellent spirit."

Yet, control-freaks can be dangerous. If only the world had never known Adolf Hitler, a megalomaniac with a craving to rule the world! Oh, the lives that could have been saved. The holocaust could have been avoided! Tyrants, dictators, and oppressors are all of the same genre. The final antichrist likely will be a control-freak who is not willing to submit to the LORD Jesus Christ.

The fact of the matter is that Jesus Christ is the King of Kings. Anyone not humble and obedient in submitting to His perfect reign will not be allowed into the Kingdom of Joy!

"Wait for the LORD and keep His way, and He will exalt you to inherit the land; you will look on when the wicked are cut off." Psalm 37:34

In the fullest sense, this is not done yet. The wicked haven't been cut off. The depraved presume their defiant direction, but the Sovereign LORD has a Day of Judgment for them.

"Fret not yourself because of evildoers; be not envious of wrongdoers!" Psalm 37:1

"See, darkness covers the earth and thick darkness is over the peoples ..."

Oh, but saints ...

"the Lord rises upon you and His glory appears over you." Isaiah 60:1-2

The LORD says to His meek people, the City of the LORD, and Zion:

*"Whereas you have been forsaken and hated ... I will make you majestic forever, a **JOY** from age to age."*
Isaiah 60:15

HAPPY ARE THOSE WHO SEEK RIGHTEOUSNESS

Happy are those who seek to please God, to be in right-standing with Him. They'll receive the Messiah, the forgiveness of their sins, the joy of salvation, and true satisfaction. Those who don't seek to follow God are lost and live in spiritual darkness.

Happy are they who are willing to repent of their sins and to turn to God. The LORD has established rules for our own well-being, our own happiness. He didn't set up the universe to be in chaos. He made it orderly. He made the spiritual world orderly, also. Happy are those who want to follow their Creator's rules.

"For God is not a God of confusion but of peace."
1 Corinthians 14:33

... BUT UNHAPPY ARE THE WICKED

The opposite of following God's rules is chaos and confusion. Observe how out of order are the lives of those who do not obey God's moral laws.

Repeatedly, "the children of Israel did evil in the sight of the Lord." Judges 2:7 NKJ

"Everyone did what was right in his own eyes." Judges 17:6

That's a catastrophe waiting to happen! The Sovereign LORD brings on catastrophes because His ways are not sought or followed.

"Disaster after disaster is reported because the whole land is destroyed." Jeremiah 4:20 HCSB

Their wicked ways yielded mayhem.

"When the wicked rise, people hide themselves, but when they perish, the righteous increase." Proverbs 28:28

We observe it in this land: the wicked rising to power, to yank control out of the hands of the righteous ones. Would we cry out for a Deliverer, a Savior to set us free?

"The wicked plots against the righteous and gnashes his teeth at him, but the Lord laughs at the wicked, for He sees that his day is coming." Psalm 37:12-13

The LORD will bring His everlasting peace to the righteous who in this world have persecution and tribulations. But, alas …

"'There is no peace,' says my God, 'for the wicked.'"

Isaiah 57:21; also see 48:22

There is no "shalom" for evil but the hope of the righteous yields the Kingdom of Peace, the New Jerusalem!

"The hope of the righteous brings joy, but the expectation of the wicked will perish." Proverbs 10:28

You can be happy, oh saints!

"Shout for JOY in the LORD, O you righteous!"
Psalm 33:1a

BLESSED ARE THE MERCIFUL

Even unbelievers experience this happiness of showing mercy toward the poor and needy. It makes them feel good. No wonder fundraising marathons are so popular. But those marathons are normally for temporary conditions. We have a further race to run as Christians. Our race is for immortal souls. Not that the physical needs of the suffering should be neglected, but the direst need for all human souls is to be reconciled to their Creator through the Messiah.

Showing mercy is compassion. It is forgiveness when needed. It is leniency when required. It is humanity. It is tenderhearted.

Cornelius was a man who extended mercy and God in return showered him with great, great mercy in sending the Apostle Peter to him.

"1 At Caesarea there was a man named Cornelius, a centurion of what was known as the Italian Cohort, 2 a devout man who feared God with all his household, gave alms generously to the people, and prayed continually to God. 3 About the ninth hour of the day he saw clearly in a vision an angel of God come in and say to him, "Cornelius." 4 And he stared at him in terror and said, 'What is it, Lord?' And he said to him, 'Your prayers and your alms have ascended as a memorial before God. 5 And now send men to Joppa and bring one Simon who is called Peter.'" Acts 10

Cornelius, because of his mercy, was sent an angel of the LORD, an apostle, and the Holy Spirit! What great mercy has our God! "His mercy endures forever."

Being merciful means to forgive. Let us remember the Word of the LORD in regards to forgiveness:

"…and forgive us our debts, as we also have forgiven our debtors." Matthew 6:12

"Christ died for the ungodly" and forgave us all. (Romans 5:6) Our sin of outright rebellion against Him, He forgave. We should likewise forgive from the heart.

"Be merciful, even as your Father is merciful." Luke 6:36

… BUT UNHAPPY ARE THE CRUEL

The atrocities that are happening in our days! The beheading of the Christians, the rape of precious little ones, and the flagrant unholy deeds of the flesh, are enough to "wear down the saints." The wicked have a Judgment Day on which they will have to answer for the cruelties down by them.

"For the day is near, the day of the LORD is near; it will be a day of clouds, a time of doom for the nations." Ezekiel 30:3

"For judgment is without mercy to one who has shown no mercy." James 2:13a

The cruel are miserable and wretched NOW. Darkness begets darkness.

The Words of our Savior: "but if your eye is bad, your whole body will be full of darkness. If then the light in you is darkness, how great is the darkness!" Matthew 6:23

"But whoever hates his brother is in the darkness and walks in the darkness, and does not know where he is going, because the darkness has blinded his eyes." 1 John 2:11

A cruel man is unhappy, though he may put up a good front.

"A man who is kind benefits himself, but a cruel man hurts himself." Proverbs 11:17

A wicked man, more than likely, has many issues. There may be many unsavory memories from childhood that go back to demonic "familiar spirits" whirring around him. May the LORD release those bound in darkness to the Light itself. That would be merciful.

"Mercy triumphs over judgment."
James 2:13b

"Give praise, O ye heavens, for the Lord hath shown mercy: shout with **JOY**, ye ends of the earth."
Isaiah 44:23 DRB

HAPPY ARE THE PURE

"And everyone who thus hopes in Him purifies himself as He is pure."
1 John 3:3

That hope is Christ. All who have this hope in them will purify himself. The pure will be able to see God.

"Who shall ascend the hill of the LORD? And who shall stand in His holy place? He who has clean hands and a pure heart, who does not lift up his soul to what is false and does not swear deceitfully." Psalm 24:4

The pure in heart are not idolaters, but their love is for the LORD.

"The pure in heart are happy; for they shall see God. Here holiness and happiness are fully described and put together. The heart must be purified by faith, and kept for God. Create in me such a clean heart, O God. None but the pure are capable of seeing God, nor would heaven be happiness to the impure. As God cannot endure to look upon their iniquity, so they cannot look upon his purity." *Matthew Henry Commentary*

God is holy. God the Father has no part of sin. Thank goodness for God the Son, who became "sin for us" to crush the roots of it. He sent His Holy Spirit to enable us to defeat sin. We now are presentable and righteous to enter before the holiness of the Father. So the pure will see YHWH God in His glory!

"For our sake He made Him to be sin who knew no sin, so that in Him we might become the righteousness of God." 2 Corinthians 5:21

Jesus Christ, as the King of Kings, is seen by Isaiah.

"And I said: 'Woe is me! For I am lost; for I am a man of unclean lips, and I dwell in the midst of a people of unclean lips; for my eyes have seen the King, the LORD of hosts!'" Isaiah 6:5

Isaiah had unclean lips. A seraph cleansed the prophet's lips with a burning coal. He lived in a land of unclean lips. We live in a land of unclean lips. Who is willing to forego the repulsive gossip? Be a blessing, not a curse. Who is willing to clean up their foul language to dwell with the LORD?

"And the tongue is a fire, a world of unrighteousness... but no human being can tame the tongue. It is a restless evil, full of deadly poison." James 3:6

"Then I will purify the lips of the peoples, that all of them may call on the name of the LORD and serve Him shoulder to shoulder." Zephaniah 3:9 NIV

The lips of all will be purified. It's a holy people who will have the privilege of being blessed by the King!

"'Therefore go out from their midst, and be separate from them, says the Lord, and touch no unclean thing; then I will welcome you, and I will be a father to you, and you shall be sons and daughters to me, says the Lord Almighty.' Therefore, since we have these promises, dear friends, let us purify ourselves from everything that contaminates body and spirit, perfecting holiness out of reverence for God." 2 Corinthians 6:17 - 7:1

"Since it is written, 'You shall be holy, for I am holy.'" 1 Peter 1:16

Your children should be holy as well.

We can see this purity of heart sometimes in innocent children who have been nurtured in a Godly home, knowing right from wrong and willing to please their parents and God their Father. These pure little hearts are happy hearts. Oh, how sad it is to see children having to deal with sinful things that they should know nothing about! Oh, that we would protect our children in their innocence!

I remember once sitting in a service near a family with young children. The pastor mentioned something in his sermon about the evil in the world. The boy looked up at his parents and asked him what he meant. Afterward, I commended those parents for protecting their children.

Let the children be happy in their innocence while they are children. They don't need to know about the extremes of evil at such a tender age. Of course, they should be taught about not speaking to strangers and such. Parents should speak with them about sins but please let your children enjoy their childhood! Shield them from the evils of the world as long as possible.

Children need to be nurtured with care. We wouldn't plant a garden without removing the briers, thorns, and weeds. Why do we think it okay to leave our impressionable children in places where they are taught other people's values? Sin is not sin, but just a disorder? Witchcraft and perversion are just alternative lifestyles?

God gave the parents the responsibility to raise up children in the way they should go.

> *"4 We will not hide them from their children, but tell to the coming generation the glorious deeds of the LORD, and his might, and the wonders that he has done. 5 He established a testimony in Jacob and appointed a law in Israel, which he commanded our fathers to teach to their children, 6 that the next generation might know them, the children yet unborn, and arise and tell them to their children, 7 so that they should set their hope in God and not forget the works of God, but keep his commandments; 8 and that they should not be like their fathers, a stubborn and rebellious generation, a generation whose heart was not steadfast, whose spirit was not faithful to God."* Psalm 78

My granddaughter, age five, just gave her heart to the LORD. She expressed her desire to never be without the LORD. Oh, how sweet!

But how many children are raised to rebel? How many children are falling prey to the ravages of sin?

It is a parent's God-given responsibility to teach children right from wrong and to help them be discerning. Why would we allow our children to listen to music with blatantly erotic lyrics? Why would we allow them to watch shows about vampires and werewolves and witchcraft? Even cartoons need to be monitored. Many are not so innocent. Many are violent or teach rebellion and witchcraft.

One day, when my children were young, they were watching a popular cartoon with superheroes. I heard a character proclaim, "Praise the sorceress!" I went to that TV and shut it off. Well, that was the last time they watched that show. I began to scrutinize the cartoons and found that many, many were filled with ungodliness.

Is it good for children to be caught up in a world of sorcery, to be filling their minds with witchcraft that is presented as laudable?

"For rebellion is as the sin of witchcraft, and stubbornness is as iniquity and idolatry." 1 Samuel 15:23a (KJ)

Our LORD taught us to pray "Your kingdom come, Your will be done." (Matthew 6:10) Witchcraft is the opposite. It stands for "my will be done." It is the operation of the flesh.

I had a mother lament to me that she didn't know where she had gone wrong. She had homeschooled her daughter and they went to a Bible-believing church. Why had she suddenly rebelled? In the same conversation, she mentioned that her daughter voraciously read a popular series of books which extolled witchcraft. There was her answer. Nowadays, one better know what your child is reading.

I frequently hear from mothers and from children that the schools are giving them books to read with all kinds of sinfulness in them, especially witchcraft. The more sensitive children might even have nightmares from reading such. Just yesterday, a young girl let me know about a book that disturbed her. I told her to tell her teacher respectfully that her God does not want her reading that book. But parents need to speak out. Because enough parents do not speak out, your children are being fed some most unsavory fare.

The Scripture encourages us to think on things that are pure.

"Finally, brothers and sisters, whatever is true, whatever is noble, whatever is right, whatever is pure, whatever is lovely, whatever is admirable—if anything is excellent or praiseworthy—think about such things. Whatever you have learned or received or heard from me, or seen in me—put it into practice. And the God of peace will be with you." Philippians 4:8-9

There are countless classic books that uphold good values. There are many good historical fiction novels written by Christians. Encourage your child that their Christianity does not stop when they go to school or when they close the Bible. They need to learn that the world will always be tempting them to compromise their values. We are called to be salt. We are called to be pure.

"Religion that is pure and undefiled before God, the Father, is this: ... to keep oneself unstained from the world." James 1:27

Help your children be pure, by keeping them unblackened from sin. Shield your precious children. Teach them the love of God from the beginning. Teach them about Jesus and the Word. Teach them right from wrong. Teach them about the forgiveness of God in Christ, so that when they do realize they have sinned, they will immediately repent and be born again!

I was raised in a Catholic school and church. While Bible study was rare, we did learn about Jesus Christ and the Ten Commandments. One day, when I was about five, I stole a 25-cent toy from a department store. I was so convicted by the Holy Spirit that I went home and cried and cried for God to forgive me, which He did. The LORD showed me many years later that this was when I was born again. And even though I strayed later due to a lack of training in the Word, the LORD did bring me back to Him!

So "teach your children well."

"The aim of our charge is love that issues from a pure heart and a good conscience and a sincere faith." 1 Timothy 1:5

"But the wisdom from above is first pure…" James 3:17

… BUT UNHAPPY ARE THE OBSCENE

The obscene abound.

We were walking in Key West, out in public. Well, I couldn't believe my eyes! I had to cover the eyes of my daughter, my 20-ish-year-old daughter, to the things that she could've seen!

It's a shame that my generation led to the downfall of society. I blame a lot on television. It used to be that there was a time when one could call the federal government and get a show cautioned for its obscenities. Now, everything seems allowed. Obscenities abound.

We fired the cable company. Not much good comes over it anymore. Sitcoms that used to be family-oriented have much perversion and rebellion. Now, we see only what we want through subscriptions.

So lawlessness abounds. The lawless are not happy. They are grumpy, cantankerous, and bad-tempered. Maybe they didn't have a happy childhood. Maybe they didn't know right from wrong. We pray for them.

"The precepts of the LORD are right, giving JOY to the heart."

Psalm 19:8

HAPPY ARE THE PERSECUTED

"Present afflictions tend also to heighten future joy."
Spurgeon's *Morning Devotional* (Numbers 11:11)

"Remember the word that I said to you: 'A servant is not greater than his master.' If they persecuted me, they will also persecute you. If they kept my word, they will also keep yours." John 15:20

Happy are the persecuted? Now, this *is* an oxymoron - to the world!

Any reading of the Acts of the Apostles will show that the gospel is not always well received by the status quo. Some political leaders, whose real agenda is their own welfare and position, want to control the populace for their own benefit. Some religious leaders are threatened by a gospel that declares we can go boldly before the throne of God Almighty without their intervention. Unscrupulous greedy business people making money off sin and vice do not want anyone liberating their captives. Yet the gospel of Jesus Christ declares,

"So if the Son sets you free, you will be free indeed." John 8:36

The high priest of the Sanhedrin forbade the apostles not to teach in Jesus' name. That was definitely upsetting the status quo. But Peter and the apostles answered, "We must obey God rather than men." Acts 5:29

"Then they [the apostles] left the presence of the council, rejoicing that they were counted worthy to suffer dishonor for the name." Acts 5:41

Rejoicing? They were rejoicing!

The apostles all were persecuted. All but John was eventually martyred. But the truth sets one free even beyond the fear of death. Saints are dying around the world daily for the name and love of Christ. I pray God's glory to rest upon them as it did for Stephen, the first Christian martyr.

"But he, full of the Holy Spirit, gazed into heaven and saw the glory of God, and Jesus standing at the right hand of God. And he said, 'Behold, I see the heavens opened, and the Son of Man standing at the right hand of God.'" Acts 7:55-56

God's grace is amazing! On one hand, Stephen is in the midst of an angry crowd threatening his life, but **he sees Jesus Christ!**

"Therefore, holy brothers and sisters, who share in the heavenly calling, fix your thoughts on Jesus, whom we acknowledge as our apostle and high priest." Hebrews 3:1 (NIV)

Let us look to Jesus under persecution. As songwriter Helen H. Lemmel wrote in 1922,

"Turn your eyes upon Jesus,
Look full in His wonderful face,
And the things of earth will grow strangely dim,
In the light of His glory and grace."

"Looking to Jesus, the founder and perfecter of our faith, who for the joy that was set before Him endured the cross, despising the shame, and is seated at the right hand of the throne of God." Hebrews 12:2

We, in America, have escaped the bulk of murdering persecution. Only a handful here have been killed for their Christian faith but many are being persecuted, under lawsuits and such to force us to compromise our convictions. If you're leading a life that is holy, you are bound to be persecuted. It's often with stares, accusations, heated language and cold-shoulders.

"Indeed, all who desire to live a godly life in Christ Jesus will be persecuted." 2 Timothy 3:12

I have had a few times when it was expedient to recall our LORD's words about rejoicing under persecution.

"'Blessed are you when others revile you and persecute you and utter all kinds of evil against you falsely on my account. Rejoice and be glad, for your reward is great in heaven, for so they persecuted the prophets who were before you.'" Matthew 5:11-12

In a few situations, people did not like the fact that I was sharing the Truth. They would verbally lash out at me. They'd try to provoke me with personal insults. When an unbeliever has no truthful argument, a personal insult is instead hurled.

"But rejoice insofar as you share Christ's sufferings, that you may also rejoice and be glad when His glory is revealed." 1 Peter 4:13

They were expecting to provoke me. But my response would be gentle, if not just silence. That in itself is a witness: that we can maintain composure and civility while they are ranting and raving. Ultimately, some of those same people would later find themselves in a dire situation and would come to me and ask for prayer!

"Bless those who persecute you; bless and do not curse them." Romans 12:14

We can bless the persecutors and that is a joy! The Spirit rises up in us that causes us to bless and not curse. Oh, it's only done by the Spirit of grace upon us. Grace! Grace! They need grace! We may get a Word from the LORD. We may get a word of knowledge. We may say a prayer. The Spirit of Christ and His glory is abiding on us.

"If you are insulted for the name of Christ, you are blessed, because the Spirit of glory and of God rests upon you." 1 Peter 4:13-14

We have the glory and the love of Christ Himself who is with us through trials and persecution.

This is dear to my heart. My husband, before he was a believer, was perturbed that I was taking the children to listen to a lecture on creationism versus macro-evolution. He later spoke with my teenage son, Richard. I could hear the conversation from another room. My husband asked my son mockingly, in relationship to God being the Creator, "Do you *really* believe that?" My son replied gently, "Yes, I do, Dad!"

Some years later, Richard, who was then college-age, invited us to a retreat. I replied to ask his dad because it seemed unlikely that he would go and he probably wouldn't go if I had asked him. But his father said, "Yes." The camaraderie of all at the retreat and the level-headedness of the youth made an impact on my husband. I think this was a breaking point: to see young people in love with their Creator, in serious discussions about the LORD, and to be jubilant in worship! And no, not a one of them on crazy drugs!

Sadly, persecution comes from those we love. But we are reminded to "pray for those who persecute you." (Matthew 5:44)

Jesus Christ aptly spoke:

"51 Do you think that I have come to give peace on earth? No, I tell you, but rather division. 52 For from now on in one house there will be five divided, three against two and two against three. 53 They will be divided, father against son and son against father, mother against daughter and daughter against mother, mother-in-law against her daughter-in-law and daughter-in-law against mother-in-law." Luke 12

We cherish the love from our family. But we owe gratitude and love to the One who gave His life for us on a wooden cross.

"Who shall separate us from the love of Christ? Shall tribulation, or distress, or persecution, or famine, or nakedness, or danger, or sword?" Romans 8:35

Despite persecutions, we rejoice because the love of Christ is our special **JOY!**

... BUT UNHAPPY ARE THE BULLIES

Ah, the bullies and tyrants have no love of Christ in them. We should pray for them. They know nothing but hate. They have no serenity. They have no goodness. They have no real joy. They have no fruit of the Spirit. (Galatians 5:19-23)

In the end, if no repentance is shown, the bullies and tyrants will know the fear of God.

"And the LORD your God will put all these curses on your foes and enemies who persecuted you." Deuteronomy 30:7

The King of Kings receives the persecuted into His sight.

"Precious in the sight of the LORD is the death of his saints." Psalm 116:15

The LORD's intent is on the righteous. He says,

"Enter into the **JOY** of your master."

Matthew 25: 23

HAPPY ARE THE PEACEMAKERS

"But the wisdom from above is first pure, then peaceable, gentle, open to reason, full of mercy and good fruits, impartial and sincere."
James 3:17

Peaceful people can diffuse angry situations with the wisdom of God. A happy, gentle person walking in the Spirit can diffuse a volatile situation.

It's Christmas Day. Some of our family, all adults, were walking downtown Dallas. Ahead of us, two men were yelling at one another, throwing suitcases around, and about to attack one another with fists. When I saw it, the Spirit of God compelled me to walk faster towards them. I called out something to the effect of "Hey, guys, it's Christmas!" I then started singing loudly, "We wish you a Merry Christmas…" Well, the two men were so shocked! They stared at me for a moment, long enough to stop the imminent fisticuffs. The song had caught them off guard! Thankfully, no blows were thrown. Oh, they still had a few angry words with one another afterward but at least no blood was spilled.

It's quite an unusual memory for us: the day granny broke up a brawl with a Christmas melody! (I don't recommend this for everyone unless so led by God!)

Bringing harmony into chaos, being a peacemaker is our calling. A spirit-controlled person does not lash out in fleshly anger, but with a supernatural gentleness.

We might want to respond in unholy and carnal outbursts. This should be avoided. Nonetheless, the Spirit does call forth a righteous anger. An example of this holy anger is when Jesus chased the money changers from the temple.

"And Jesus entered the temple and drove out all who sold and bought in the temple, and he overturned the tables of the money-changers and the seats of those who sold pigeons. He said to them, 'It is written, 'My house shall be called a house of prayer,' but you make it a den of robbers.'" Matthew 21:13

Some would claim to have "holy anger" when it is not of the Spirit. A person has received some offenses and feels justified to be angry. We are cautioned not to take offenses for they perpetrate wrath.

"Good sense makes one slow to anger, and it is his glory to overlook an offense." Proverbs 19:11

It is not necessarily a sin to be angry, but it shouldn't fester.

Paul writes:

"Be angry and do not sin; do not let the sun go down on your anger, and give no opportunity to the devil." Ephesians 4:26

The devil will come into a strained situation and bring division and strife, if wisdom is not used. The devil would have us make mountains out of molehills. We must be aware of his devious devices.

When I was a young Christian, a Bible study teacher made a comment and somehow I thought she was talking about me. I did not understand why she would be bringing up something in a class about my situation. Thankfully, the Spirit led me to ask her about it. When I did, she apologized and said that she had no idea that was my situation but was just speaking generally.

Anyway, the enemy had tried to drive a wedge between the two of us! I had taken offense where there was no intention of offense. I am glad that God directed me to speak to her about it, because I found out there was no need for offense at all! Had we allowed the enemy's scheme to divide us, that would have stolen from us the friendship we had developed. The ministry we did together might not have been and *that* ministry set many captives free!

Offense in the Church is a common tactic of the enemy and should be recognized for what it is.

A woman was quite enraged. She grew more enraged at me because she couldn't enrage me. It was something about being a "Christian" but it made no sense. She physically attacked me. I grabbed her arms to keep her from hitting me and calmly held her. It was a supernatural calm that came over me, the grace of the Spirit. She fussed and threw insults for a while until her strength left her. But I never hurt her or lashed back at her. I know God gave me the supernatural peace.

A peaceful spirit will control the flesh that wants to lash back in anger.

"A gentle answer turns away wrath, but a harsh word stirs up anger." Proverbs 15:1

"If possible, so far as it depends on you, live peaceably with all." Romans 12:18

God wants us to be at peace with our neighbors. He Himself is the great peacemaker, the God of peace: Yahweh-Shalom in Hebrew. (Judges 6:24)

In Hebrew, people say "Shalom!" which means "peace" as a greeting. Instead of just 'Hello!" or "Good-bye!", we can speak a blessing of "Peace!" to one another by saying "Shalom!"

"Blessed are the peacemakers, for they shall be called sons of God." What a privilege to be a son of God! That, in itself, is a reason to jump for joy!

As sons of God, we are called to be His ambassadors:

"… He has committed to us the word of reconciliation. Therefore, we are ambassadors for Christ, God making His appeal through us. We implore you on behalf of Christ, be reconciled to God." 2 Corinthians 5:19b-20

It is the duty of an ambassador to represent their country and be a peacemaker between men of different nations. God has offered reconciliation. His terms are clearly spelled out in the Word. We must come to the Father through the Son, Jesus Christ. This is the message we share on behalf of the King. We are to "preach Christ and Him crucified" and implore them to be reconciled, to make their peace with their Creator. (1 Corinthians 1:23)

"But in your hearts honor Christ the Lord as holy, always being prepared to make a defense to anyone who asks you for a reason for the hope that is in you; yet do it with gentleness and respect …" 1 Peter 3:15

There is hostility against the gospel. If people truly understood their condition and the mercy of God, they should come running to Jesus. But they can't see!

"In their case the god of this world has blinded the minds of the unbelievers, to keep them from seeing the light of the gospel of the glory of Christ, who is the image of God." 2 Corinthians 4:4

There are countless testimonies of people coming to Christ through the patient, persistent witness and prayers of the saints. We need to be gentle peacemakers to His Kingdom and then God can keep us in perfect peace.

"You will keep him in perfect peace, whose mind is stayed on You: because he trusts in You. Trust in Yahweh forever; for in Yah, Yahweh, is everlasting strength." (Isaiah 26:3-4)

There is abundant **JOY** in bringing someone to YAH!

… BUT UNHAPPY ARE THE HELL-RAISERS

Hell-raisers try to hinder people from coming to Christ. They lift up hell and glorify the devil and his hordes. Maybe not in an obvious way, but they do glorify the fallen. They glorify the fallen in the pro-choice movement, in the pro-homosexual movement, in the pro-satan movement.

In July 2013, at the Austin Capitol, there was a bill to protect babies in the womb from late-term abortion. Having been an eyewitness to these events, I saw malevolent, brutal evil. Evil had sway over many of the pro-abortion, pro-lust, pro-licentiousness crowd. Their rude, crude signs were vulgar and spoke volumes as to who was the chief instigator behind them. Some even chanted "Hail, satan!" Their own words reveal their evil influence! I can't even repeat the vulgarities on their signs, some even blasphemous regarding the LORD Jesus Christ.

The hell-raisers are bent on keeping those from the Kingdom of Christ's glory. And they were not happy. They were anarchists who make such a ruckus as to drown out any voice or vote that does not agree with them. They were angry people with whom it is nearly impossible to have a civilized discussion.

On another note, there are those that would cause havoc in a more mundane way. They are the mischief-makers, rabble-rousers, and gossip mongers. Gossipers are some of the most run-of-the-mill troublemakers.

"A perverse person spreads dissension, and a gossip separates the closest friends." Proverbs 16:28 NET

"A wicked scoundrel digs up evil, and his slander is like a scorching fire." Proverbs 16:27 NET

The gossipers are amongst the common everyday fiend. They, if not careful, can grow more monstrous. They can become tyrants. Gossipmongers, trouble-makers, and tyrants are only "happy" when they cause another ill. That is not true joy.

*"Deceit is in the heart of those who devise evil, but those who plan peace have **JOY**."*
Proverbs 12:20

THE JOY OF OTHERS

HAPPY ARE THE GIVERS

There is one more statement that Jesus Christ said recorded in the Book of Acts.

"It is more blessed to give than to receive." Acts 20:35

You are blessed to receive a gift, but the giver is more blessed! Our Father in heaven is a Giver and He is happy to give us the best gifts! If you want to be happy, give freely and joyfully!

"Each one must give as he has decided in his heart, not reluctantly or under compulsion, for God loves a cheerful giver." 2 Corinthians 9:7

To this point, it is my conviction based on New Testament Scriptures that Christians are NOT obligated to the 10% tithing as still taught in many churches. However, if one is walking in the Spirit and not being selfish, one's overall giving, which would include the poor and suffering, will probably EXCEED that 10%!!

If you are interested in this subject, please read the book of Galatians and Acts 15.

That being said, it is a great JOY! It's fun to give! It's a blessing to give! It's an honor to give! And if we are being changed from "glory to glory" to reflect more of our Father's character, then we will become a lavish giver.

... BUT UNHAPPY ARE THE SCROOGES

Did you ever hear of a happy Scrooge? He wasn't **JOYFUL** until he started giving!

THE JOY OF INTERCESSION

The joy of intercession is the power of prayer! When we pray for another that is a form of giving, giving in a unique way.

This was expressed to me through my recent sickness. My husband and children were praying. My church was praying. My neighbors were praying. Everybody was praying for me. People I didn't know were praying for me. And their prayers were answered. The joy of another person's happiness is shared by all who gave time to pray!

We all have enough problems. There is a never ending need for prayer: sickness, schooling, financial setbacks, mishaps, the salvation of others, ad infinitum. The need is endless. But we have a high priest.

"… He always lives to make intercession for them." Hebrews 7:25

Christ is joined by others in prayer. Are we to be a part of that intercession for others? Will we have the joy of knowing that Kingdom purposes are attained? Will we be able to share in the joy of knowing a nation is brought to Christ?

> "6 And the foreigners who join themselves to the LORD, to minister to Him, to love the name of the LORD, and to be His servants,

everyone who keeps the Sabbath and does not profane it, and holds fast my covenant—7 these I will bring to My holy mountain, and make them **joyful in My house of prayer**; their burnt offerings and their sacrifices will be accepted on My altar; for My house shall be called **a house of prayer for all peoples."** Isaiah 56:6-7

There is joy in God's house of prayer! So many times we have been in intercession and the Lord performs an amazing marvel. He takes all the crying and weeping and deep calling on the Lord and He changes it to joy!

We were in intercession, especially for a minister who had fallen, a tragic situation. We were weeping on the floor for him. After we had prayed, I went to the door of the hall and a sudden joy came upon me. It turned me from sad to a joy unspeakable. This was a supernatural experience. Another intercessor joined in, too. We both started laughing! We went to the ladies room and laughed, for we didn't want to disturb the church. I think we laughed there for fifteen minutes or more! The Lord did not want us to leave with that extreme heaviness. He wanted to lighten up the feeling and replace it with **JOY**!

Another incident happened when I was new to intercessory prayer. I was wondering if there could be any results to my prayers as I was making appeals for situations far away, particularly the persecuted church. I asked the LORD to show me a sign. Randomly, I commented that the sign should have purple in it. I got up from prayer. Next thing, I was looking at the newspaper. There was my sign. It was an article about a South American country where there were captives for Christ. They had been released! We had just prayed about that recently. And there in the photo release was the color purple! Well, I could have jumped for **JOY!**

THE PERSECUTED CHURCH

"Indeed, all who desire to live a godly life in Christ Jesus will be persecuted." 2 Timothy 3:12

The persecuted church has always been around. There are the first martyrs of the Roman era to the saints who opposed the Roman Catholic heresies to many missionaries in many lands through the centuries. I recommend <u>Foxe's Book of Martyrs</u> on this subject. The slaughter continues as led by Muslim radicals, particularly ISIS, who executes with the beheading of Christians.

"9 When he opened the fifth seal, I saw under the altar the souls of those who had been slain for the word of God and for the witness they had borne. 10 They cried out with a loud voice, 'O Sovereign Lord, holy and true, how long before you will judge and avenge our blood on those who dwell on the earth?' 11 Then they were each given a white robe and told to rest a little longer, until the number of their fellow servants and their brothers should be complete, who were to be killed as they themselves had been." Revelation 6

God knows that I don't know how to pray for this. I pray for the cruelty to stop. I pray for miracles of deliverance. I pray in tongues for the most part. Sadly, Christians will have to be killed because it does say so in the Scriptures. Perhaps we could save some in intercession. Some may be appointed for earthly salvation. Some are going to their final rest and reward. That in itself is glorious! Jesus gives the victory in all we do. Weeping and sorrow are replaced by great **JOY** in the LORD's Kingdom!

THE JOY OF TEARS

"For I will turn their mourning into **joy**."
Jeremiah 31:13

"Weeping may endure for a night but **joy** comes in the morning."
Psalm 30:5

THE JOY OF JUSTICE

"It is a **joy** for the just to do justice."
Proverbs 21:15

"You have loved righteousness and hated wickedness. Therefore God, your God, has anointed you with the oil of **gladness** beyond your companions."
Psalm 45:7

"There is **joy** for those who deal justly
with others and always
do what is right."
Psalm 106:3 NLT

JOY AT ANOTHER'S TRIUMPH

I cry at weddings. Oh, the rhapsody of love! Two people are joined in holy matrimony. They are tears of gladness. They are tears of joy for another's happiness.

We should be joyful at each other's joys in the body of Christ. We are of one body.

"But as it is, God arranged the members in the body, each one of them, as He chose." 1 Corinthians 12:18

This gives us lots of opportunity for joy! We can be joyful at another's victory, another's triumph, another's repentance, another's holiness.

St. John expressed this joy.

"I rejoiced greatly to find some of your children walking in the truth, just as we were commanded by the Father." 2 John 1:4

One of the most joyful events of my life was when my husband came to Christ. It was a distressing time, but it had eternal ramifications!

My husband came home one night and he was distraught. Nothing was going right with him. He walked in and asked for prayer. Now, my husband never, never asked for prayer! He didn't believe in it.

I wanted to jump for joy, but he was so disturbed and agitated, I knew I couldn't. I hugged him lovingly and just winked at my daughter who was sitting near. That was his moment of coming to the Truth. He accepted Jesus Christ as His Savior and has been going to church meetings ever since.

When Jesus had met with the woman at the well at Samaria, He was full of joy and brimming with the Holy Ghost.

"Meanwhile, the disciples were urging Him, saying, "Rabbi, eat." But He said to them, "I have food to eat that you do not know about." John 4:31-32

Now I don't think that Jesus stated that without enthusiasm. I think He voiced that with some gusto, "I have food to eat THAT YOU DO NOT KNOW ABOUT!" Maybe there was laughter and the joy of the Spirit. Nothing is quite like leading someone to the Lord. The Samaritan women went on to lead many in the town to the Lord.

We can pray for Nablus, the city she was in, to return to the Lord today. Nothing is too difficult for the Lord. We visited this city on my fifth trip to Israel. We prayed that once again, the Lord would bring the knowledge of Him, the Savior. Pray for Nablus, right now if you please. The Lord did it once! May He do it again! May we share the **JOY** of another's salvation in Jesus Christ.

THE JOY OF THE HARVEST

"You have multiplied the nation
and increased its **joy**;
They rejoice before You according
to the **joy** of the harvest."
Isaiah 9:3

"Those who sow in tears shall reap in **JOY**.
He who continually goes forth weeping,
bearing seed for sowing,
shall doubtless come again with rejoicing,
bringing his sheaves with him."
Psalm 126:5-6

"Already the one who reaps is receiving wages and gathering fruit for eternal life, so that sower and reaper may **rejoice** together."
John 4:36

THE JOY OF LOVE

THE JOY OF LOVE

*"If you keep my commandments, you will abide in my love, just as I have kept my Father's commandments and abide in His love. These things I have spoken to you, that my **joy** may be in you, and that your **joy may be full**."*

John 15:10-11

The joy of love! Full joy! The little melody sums this up:

"This is my commandment that you love one another that your joy may be full. That your joy may be full ..."

This is "agape" love, a divine love, a self-sacrificing love. Agape love means 'good will'. God was full of good will towards us that He sent His Son and announced it with:

"Glory to God in the highest, and on earth peace, **good will** toward men." Luke 2:14

God so loved the world! He was full of good will towards us that He didn't want to abandon us to the satanic system. God sent His Redeemer!

When we show forth this kind of love, a self-sacrificing love, our joy if full!

"So if there is any encouragement in Christ, any comfort from love, any participation in the Spirit, any affection and sympathy, complete my **joy** by being of the same mind, having the same love, being in full accord and of one mind. Do nothing from selfish ambition or conceit, but in humility count others more significant than yourselves. Let each of you look not only to his own interests, but also to the interests of others. Have this mind among yourselves, which is yours in Christ Jesus ... He humbled Himself by becoming obedient to the point of death, even death on a cross." Philippians 2:1-5, 8

How often do we "look not only to his own interests, but also to the interests of others"? Today's culture is "I deserve a break today."

"Love is patient, love is kind. It does not envy, it does not boast, it is not proud." 1 Corinthians 13:4

Love does not stir up strife and discord with gossip.

"And above all things have fervent love for one another, for love will cover a multitude of sins." 1 Peter 4:8

Love covers the sin, bringing it only to the attention of those who need to know about it, in the case of parents and authorities. Certain idiosyncrasies about a person should never be mentioned for it protects their character. Certain sins of the past should not be divulged. "Treat other people as you'd like them to treat you!"

"Hatred stirs up strife, but love covers all offenses." Proverbs 10:12

Love doesn't whisper behind closed doors at another's troubles. But love does "brings back a sinner from his wandering."

"Let him know that whoever brings back a sinner from his wandering will save his soul from death and will cover a multitude of sins." James 5:20

Sinful habits need to be broken. One may need deliverance from evil strongholds through prayer. But God's grace is there for our total transformation. Not to speak the truth is denying people the freedom to be who God made them to be in Christ! As any parent should know, sometimes love must be tough. Is it wise love to allow a child to do anything they feel like doing, knowing the consequences could destroy them? We love them, but caution against wrong.

Someone said it this way: we need to differentiate between the "WHO" and the "DO". We love the "WHO" but cannot condone bad "DO"s. God's law of love instructs us to love the sinner, and hate the sin. But the Scripture tells us often to "hate evil."

"The fear of the LORD is hatred of evil." Proverbs 8:13a

"Abhor what is evil." Romans 12:9b

Evil hurts people. EVIL HURTS PEOPLE. That's a bad "DO." Love wants the best, for people to be safe and happy and free, in the truest sense of these words. Hating evil is necessary for the good will of people everywhere. Love hates evil. And when evil is destroyed, there is **JOY!**

THE JOY OF BATTLE

*"Let them ever **shout for joy**."*
Psalm 5:11

Why do warriors go to battle? Love or lack of love could be the motive. Shielding one against an enemy with nefarious intent **is love**. We pray now for those who are soldiers, policeman, fireman, and anyone who is a first-line of defense against evil. These go to battle because there is a need for the good of all, and it is an act of love.

But when the battle is over, there is joy! When evil is destroyed, there is **joy!**

"5 Let the Godly exult in glory;

let them sing for **JOY** on their beds.

6 Let the high praises of God be in their throats

and two-edged swords in their hands,

7 to execute vengeance on the nations

and punishments on the peoples,

8 to bind their kings with chains

and their nobles with fetters of iron,

9 to execute on them the judgment written!

This is honor for all his Godly ones.

Praise the LORD!"

Psalm 149

This right have all the saints! The joy should come BEFORE the victory. Have faith and joy before the triumph is manifest! This is seen in the Book of Esther. Haman's plot was to destroy all the Jews. Due to Esther's love for her people, the Jews had the king's edict, granting them the right to destroy and kill those who were sworn against them.

"The Jews had light and gladness, joy and honor." Esther 8:16

This was BEFORE the day of Purim, the day of celebration of their success.

Israeli men told me they were confident of their victory against the wicked foes of vehement Islam. There would be costly casualties, but the Jews were nonetheless assured of their total victory and of them living in peace. This is the fact that the LORD said:

"But the meek shall inherit the land and delight themselves in abundant peace." Psalm 37:11

The LORD Himself will descend to protect them! And that will be a triumphal **JOY!**

THE JOY OF BEING IN HIS WILL

"Jesus answered them, 'This is the work of God, that you believe in Him whom He has sent.'"
John 6:29

This is the work, the will of God: to be in fellowship with Him! If one doesn't start with that, it's pointless. One must believe! One must come into communion with the grace of God.

"If you love Me, you will keep My commandments." John 14:15

How much one loves God is determined by how much we live in holiness. After one is a believer, and one is being sanctified, what God may want for your particular life may vary. There are different chores for each of us, but we are part of one Body.

"Now there are varieties of gifts, but the same Spirit; and there are varieties of service, but the same Lord; and there are varieties of activities, but it is the same God who empowers them all in everyone. To each is given the manifestation of the Spirit for the common good."

1 Corinthians 12:4-7

The common good. But all is for the Body of Christ. We are to **joyfully** fulfill our callings and our destinies as saints.

Some of us may need to suffer the loss of property, such as those saints being hijacked by the courts these days. "Politically-correct" judges demand they pay through the nose. They make cake bakeries and photographers out to be malicious because they don't go along with licentiousness. "Politically-correct" is often "politically- corrupt."

"… and you **joyfully** accepted the plundering of your property, since you knew that you yourselves had a better possession and an abiding one." Hebrews 10:34

Yes, we do have an everlasting possession! We are to rejoice! Paul would eventually be martyred but he understood it as a cause to be glad!

"Even if I am to be poured out as a drink offering upon the sacrificial offering of your faith, I am glad and **rejoice** with you all. Likewise, you also should be glad and **rejoice** with me." Philippians 2:17-18

"**REJOICE** always." 1 Thessalonians 5:16

"REJOICED EXCEEDINGLY WITH GREAT JOY"

The Sovereign LORD has everything in control. From time immortal, the Lamb was "slain from the foundation of the world." The precise moment of Emmanuel's nativity on the earth was intended. And God prepared some unusual vessels for their visit to see the King of Kings.

"When they saw the star, they **rejoiced** exceedingly with great **joy**." Matthew 2:10

They're on their way with gifts of gold, frankincense and myrrh. The wise men rejoiced when they had seen the star, the sign of the Messiah.

They "rejoiced exceedingly with great joy."

"ἐχάρησαν χαρὰν μεγάλην σφόδρα"

(G5463 + G5479 + G3173 + G4970)

G5463 "chairo" means "glad for grace"

G5479 "chara" means "grace recognized"

G3173 means "in the widest sense"

G4970 means "done to the max"

The wise men were *"glad for grace,"* and *"grace recognized," "in the widest sense," "done to the max!"*

The Magi were ecstatic! They were doubly glad!

My point in this is that "joy" or "chara" is "grace recognized." How often we do not recognize the grace we have! The grace of the LORD in salvation is beyond measure! If joy is "grace recognized," then we Christians have **joy a-plenty!**

Here are some root words for cognate "chara":

"For from His fullness we have all received, **grace** upon **grace**." John 1:16

"In Him, we have redemption through His blood, the forgiveness of our trespasses, according to the riches of His **grace**." Ephesians 1:7

So, therefore, if we have **grace**, we should have overflowing **JOY**!

THE GIFT OF THE MAGI

What a JOY to do the will of the LORD! The wise men were excited to see the star because they will behold the Messiah. They gave a gift of gold which may be how they survived in Egypt. Additionally, these gifts of gold, frankincense, and myrrh were symbolic.

Gold is to crown Him for He is the King of Kings.

"Then I looked, and behold, a white cloud, and seated on the cloud one like a Son of Man, **with a golden crown on his head**, and a sharp sickle in his hand." Revelation 14:14

His High Priestly role commanded frankincense.

"For we do not have a **High Priest** who is unable to sympathize with our weaknesses, but one who in every respect has been tempted as we are, yet without sin." Hebrews 4:15

Myrrh was for His death. His "sorrowing, sighing, bleeding, dying"[5] as the one sufficient sacrifice required for mankind's atonement.

"But when Christ had offered for all time a **single sacrifice** for sins, He sat down at the right hand of God." Hebrews 10:12

---

[5] Words to "We Three Kings", John H. Hopkins, 1857

Such a sacrifice! We can never express our sentiments over this offering of love! It is "grace recognized" and for that we shout for **JOY!**

THE STAR OF BETHLEHEM

On June 30th, 2015, the Star of Bethlehem re-appeared after a roughly 2000 year hiatus.

"15b ...The oracle of Balaam the son of Beor, the oracle of the man whose eye is opened, 16 the oracle of him who hears the words of God, and knows the knowledge of the Most High, who sees the vision of the Almighty, falling down with his eyes uncovered: 17 I see Him, but not now; I behold Him, but not near: **a star shall come out of Jacob**, and a scepter shall rise out of Israel; it shall crush the forehead of Moab and break down all the sons of Sheth. 18 Edom shall be dispossessed; Seir also, his enemies, shall be dispossessed. Israel is doing valiantly. 19 And one from Jacob shall exercise dominion and destroy the survivors of cities!" (Numbers 24:15b-19)

The Star of Bethlehem proclaimed the LORD's nativity. Is this part of the "great signs from heaven" to signal the LORD's return? (Luke 21:11) The slayings of Christians has already begun.

"But before all this they will lay their hands on you and persecute you ..." Luke 21:12

"And I looked, and behold, a pale horse! And its rider's name was Death, and Hades followed him. And they were given authority over a fourth of the earth, to kill <u>with sword</u> and with famine and with pestilence and by wild beasts of the earth." Revelation 6:8

The slaughter of Christians is prophetic. It says so in the Word. But the LORD is returning!

We can only say, "the Spirit and the Bride say, 'Come.'" Revelation 22:17a

"Let us **rejoice** and exult and give Him the glory, for the marriage of the Lamb has come, and His Bride has made herself ready;" Revelation 19:7

*"Rejoice in the Lord always; again I will say, **REJOICE.**"*

Philippines 4:4

The JOY OF JOYS

THE HOLY PRESENCE OF GOD

"One thing have I asked of the LORD, that will I seek after: that I may dwell in the house of the LORD all the days of my life, to gaze upon the beauty of the LORD and to inquire in is temple."

Psalm 27:4

"Then I will go to the altar of God,
to God my **exceeding joy**, and
I will praise you with the lyre,
O God, my God."

Psalm 43:4

"For You make him most blessed forever.
You make him glad with the
joy of Your presence."

Psalm 21:6

"But the righteous shall be glad; they shall exult before God; they shall be
jubilant with joy!"

Psalm 68:3

> "And He said, "My presence will go with you, and I will give you rest."
> Exodus 33:14

JOY JOYS!

> *"Whom having not seen, ye love; in whom, though now ye see Him not, yet believing, ye rejoice with **joy unspeakable** and full of glory:"* 1 Peter 1:8 (KJV)

The LORD is coming back someday in glory and majesty and splendor.

"Who is like You, O LORD, among the gods? Who is like You, majestic in holiness, awesome in glorious deeds, doing wonders?" Exodus 15:11

He is holy.

"Holy, holy, holy, is the Lord God Almighty, who was and is and is to come!" Revelation 4:8b

He is the "I AM that I AM." He is YHWH. (Exodus 3:14)

He is worthy.

"Worthy are you, our Lord and God, to receive glory and honor and power, for You created all things, and by your will they existed and were created." Revelation 4:11

We are "waiting for our blessed hope, the appearing of the glory of our great God and Savior Jesus Christ." Titus 2:13

"What a day that will be when my Jesus I shall see!"[6]

Oh, the day we meet Him face to face!

"Beloved, we are God's children now, and what we will be has not yet appeared; but we know that when He appears we shall be like Him, because we shall see Him as He is." 1 John 3:2

We shall be changed! Raptured up! When He appears we will be transformed! We are going to be like Him!

THE PRESENCE

But for now, we will enjoy His Presence in the spiritual realm, as much as we have grace. The Holy Presence enters in. It is undeniable and unquestionable.

David knew it.

"You make known to me the path of life; in your presence there is **fullness of joy**; at your right hand are pleasures forevermore." Psalm 16:11

The Israelites knew it.

---

[6] *Written by Jim Hall*

"And when all the people saw the pillar of cloud standing at the entrance of the tent, all the people would rise up and worship, each at his tent door." Exodus 33:10

"So that the priests could not stand to minister because of the cloud, for **the glory of the LORD filled** the house of the LORD." 1 Kings 8:11

People of old knew the Presence, the Holy Spirit: He is the resonance of joy! He is the *Ruach HaKo'dosh*.

The apostles knew it particularly on the Day of Pentecost.

"When the day of Pentecost came, they were all together in one place. Suddenly a sound like the blowing of a violent wind came from heaven and filled the whole house where they were sitting. They saw what seemed to be tongues of fire that separated and came to rest on each of them. All of them were filled with the Holy Spirit and began to speak in other tongues as the Spirit enabled them." Acts 2:1-4

"And Peter said to them, 'Repent and be baptized every one of you in the name of Jesus Christ for the forgiveness of your sins, and you will **receive the gift of the Holy Spirit. For the promise is for you and for your children and for all who are far off, everyone whom the Lord our God calls to Himself.**'" Acts 2:38-39

The promise is for you! The Holy Spirit is for you! His effect, His fruit is to generate goodness in spirit, soul, and body! His effect is **JOY!**

THE SPIRIT'S EFFECT

"If the Spirit of Him who raised Jesus from the dead dwells in you, He who raised Christ Jesus from the dead will also give life to your mortal bodies through his Spirit who dwells in you."

Romans 8:11

The Holy Spirit is the pledge of a fuller life in the Spirit and of things to come, when "this mortal body must put on immortality." 1 Corinthians 15:53

God has "put His seal on us and given us His Spirit in our hearts as a guarantee." 2 Corinthians 1:22

"… so that what is mortal will be swallowed up by life. He who has prepared us for this very thing is God, who has given us the Spirit as a guarantee." 2 Corinthians 5:4b-5

But while we are still mortal, if one is born-again, we *do* have the Spirit of God indwelling us. We are spirit beings, too.

Therefore, the Church can know His Presence, too, in the spirit realm. The stumbling block can be that we walk too much in the flesh and not in the Spirit.

"The spirit indeed is willing, but the flesh is weak." Mark 14:38

"Did you receive the Spirit by works of the law or by hearing with faith? Are you so foolish? Having begun by the

Spirit, are you now being perfected by the flesh?" Galatians 3:2b-3

"That which is born of the flesh is flesh, and that which is born of the Spirit is spirit." John 3:6

It would be an impossibility for the flesh to give birth to a spirit! The new birth in the Spirit is what makes our lives different, transforming us to see realities in Christ!

"These things God has revealed to us through the Spirit. For the Spirit searches everything, even the depths of God." 1 Corinthians 2:10

Would we go deeper with God! He can take us to spirit venues, to know the mysteries and secrets of God.

There is a prophetic word for me that I will hear the stars singing the praise of the LORD. How wonderful would that be! For now, I know by faith, but then I'll see:

"Sing for **JOY**, O heavens, and exult, O earth; break forth, O mountains, into singing! For the LORD has comforted His people and will have compassion on His afflicted." Isaiah 49:13

We will hear wisdom from the LORD, from His Holy Spirit.

"For we walk by faith, not by sight." 2 Corinthians 5:7

"Hear, O my people, and I will speak …" Psalm 50:7

If we are walking in the Spirit, the Holy Spirit of God can lift one up and make one to shine like Jesus! Would we all become more like Him in love and in kindness, in mercies and in grace, in discernment and in wisdom, and in holiness and in faithfulness! May the world realize the Kingdom of God that we **share** and by whom we share it! Walking in the Spirit, may we arise and shine and invite others into the Kingdom of **JOY!**

"I will make you an eternal excellence, a joy of many generations."
Isaiah 60:15 NKJ

THE HELPER

The Holy Spirit of God is called our Helper, our Comforter.

"But the Helper, the Holy Spirit, whom the Father will send in My name, He will teach you all things and bring to your remembrance all that I have said to you." John 14:26

"But when the Helper comes, whom I will send to you from the Father, the Spirit of truth, who proceeds from the Father, He will bear witness about Me." John 15:26

All of us born-again believers have the Helper, but some keep Him airtight. They don't allow Him to be seen.

"Or do you not know that your body is a temple of the Holy Spirit within you, whom you have from God?" 1 Corinthians 6:19a

We must remember that the Helper is in other Christians, even those we don't care for that much.

"Do nothing from selfish ambition or conceit, but in humility count others more significant than yourselves." Philippians 2:3

His Spirit is within us, collectively. He dwells in **all of us**. The mutual joy that comes from the Body of Christ is glorious! A meeting where everyone is focused on the LORD is fulfilling and fruitful. The Holy Spirit *in all of us* greets us with **JOY!**

The Holy Spirit maximizes and magnifies in us as we learn to reject flesh and walk in the Spirit. The Helper should be evident amongst us. His life <u>in us</u> is **JOY!**

THE PARAKLÉTOS

As I grew in the LORD, I wanted to live my life according to the Scriptures. Sometimes I wasn't correct about what that meant, but I tried. Sometimes I was overly keen in trying to do things right. But my desire was to live by the Scriptures. I didn't do this because I needed to "win" heaven. I was already born again and alive in God's Kingdom. But I did it because I was thankful. I owed my life to the Savior on Calvary. I did it out of love for Him who showed me grace and mercy. I wanted to please Him.

"If you love Me, you will keep my commandments." John 14:15

Jesus continues in this homily as if to say the Holy Spirit is the key.

"And I will ask the Father, and He will give you another Helper, to be with you forever, even the Spirit of truth, whom the world cannot receive, because it neither sees Him nor knows Him. You know Him, for He dwells with you and will be in you." John 14:16-17

We who have been born again recognize the Spirit of God, the Spirit of Truth. He is the Advocate, the Paraklétos. He reveals the "right judgment calls,"[7] if we listen to Him, just as an attorney is able to make "right judgment calls." The Paraklétos knows the Law and He knows the Law of Love. The Spirit recognizes what is right and wrong.

If we listen to the Holy Spirit and the Scriptures, He teaches us. Sometimes we are too swayed by the flesh and demonic influences to get a rightful picture. But God knows how to change us. Sometimes it's more quickly. Sometimes it's slowly. His Spirit moves in us as we grow to be Christ-like.

As John the Baptist said, "He must increase, but I must decrease." John 3:30

Would this be the prayer for all Christians! "He must increase, but I must decrease." We would be saving the world for Jesus if this were the case!

---

[7] Copyright © 1987, 2011 by Helps Ministries, Inc.

We are called to be saints. The saints stand apart and are holy. Alas, some Christians don't follow the Spirit exclusively "but the cares of the world and the deceitfulness of riches choke the word" of God out. (Matthew 13:22) They will be saved, but they will suffer loss.

"11 For no one can lay a foundation other than that which is laid, which is Jesus Christ. 12 Now if anyone builds on the foundation with gold, silver, precious stones, wood, hay, straw— 13 each one's work will become manifest, for the Day will disclose it, because it will be revealed by fire, and the fire will test what sort of work each one has done. 14 If the work that anyone has built on the foundation survives, he will receive a reward. 15 If anyone's work is burned up, he will suffer loss, though he himself will be saved, but only as through fire." 1 Corinthians 3

The straw and hay won't last. Let us be faithful to the LORD in building with precious jewels, silver, and gold. The Paraklétos is always accessible.

"Call to me and I will answer you, and will tell you great and hidden things that you have not known." Jeremiah 33:3

"He must increase, but I must decrease."

That is true **JOY!**

THE GODHEAD

*"Where is He who put in the midst of them
His Holy Spirit?"*
Isaiah 63:11

The Holy Spirit is divine. He is part of the Godhead.

YHWH is the Father Almighty in heaven.

"And because you are sons, God has sent the Spirit of His Son into our hearts, crying, 'Abba! Father!'" Galatians 4:6

Jesus Christ is He who lived amongst us. He is "God with us," Emmanuel.

"For in Him [Christ], the whole fullness of deity dwells bodily." Colossians 2:9

And Christ will come again!

The **Holy Spirit** is He who is with us now. He is abiding in us.

"You, however, are not in the flesh, but in the Spirit, if in fact the Spirit of God dwells in you. Anyone who does not have the Spirit of Christ does not belong to Him." Romans 8:9

He comes to live in our hearts the moment we have faith in the Savior Jesus Christ. He inspires us. He gives true believers zest and zing and **JOY** now!

"YOUR LIGHT DO WE SEE LIGHT"

Christians see the Father, Son, and Holy Spirit in the Godhead. They are one and the same. There are not three Gods. The Godhead is one. We find this in Psalm 36.

"For with You is the fountain of life; in Your light do we see light." Psalm 36:9

"God is Light." John 8:12; 1 John 1:5

God is the True Light, not the light coming from your light bulb. But God made physical light and we can learn things about God from studying physical light. Just as we can learn things about people by observing the things they write and create, we can learn things about God from studying His Word and His creation.

"In Him was life, and the life was the Light of men." John 1:4

Jesus is "the True Light, who gives light to everyone..." John 1:9

So what can we learn about the True Light from His creation of physical light? What is physical light? Scientists have been trying to figure that out for years just as theologians have been trying to understand God, the True Light, for many years!

Physical light is very hard to describe and understand. Scientists say now that light is both a "wave" (like sound waves or radio waves) and a "particle" (a tiny bit of matter) and also something mysterious that "cannot be fully imagined"! [8] If the smartest scientists cannot fully understand physical light, is it any wonder that we have a hard time understanding God who is the True Light?

Light which is ONE thing actually acts as three things all at the same time: wave, particle, and an unknown something.

In the same way, YHWH God is ONE God and yet Father, Son, and Spirit!

Did you know that physical light has parts that are NOT visible to the human eye? We can only see part of what light really and wholly is. This part we see is called "visible light."

Likewise, Yeshua or Jesus Christ, the Son of God, is the part of God that we can see! He is the visible part when He chooses to be seen! Jesus walked on the earth amongst men, two thousand years ago, and appeared throughout the Bible to some people, and sometimes people see Him spiritually in visions and dreams. Today, many people in places where they will not allow Christian missionaries are having visions of Christ in the spirit! Someday, Jesus the Messiah will return and the Bible says that "every eye will see Him!" Revelation 1:7

Yes, Jesus Christ is "the image of the invisible God" Colossians 1:15

---

[8] *http://en.wikipedia.org/wiki/Light (See Quantum Theory section)*

Jesus is the visible part of God, but there's still the big, vast invisible part! This helps to explain why Jesus said, "the Father is greater than I." John 14:28

The Greek word for "greater" is "megas." Something bigger is "mega." The vastness of light is bigger than the smaller part we can actually see. YHWH God is bigger than what we can see of Him. He's more than the appearance of the Son. Yet Jesus is still FULLY GOD! He's all True Light!

Visible light is still light and is ONE with the rest of light, not separate. Visible or invisible, light is light! It's all the same thing or substance. Likewise, the Son of God IS God and is also ONE with God.

"...and the Word was with God, and the Word was God." Jesus is both with God and God!

Jesus said, "I and my Father are one." John 10:30

Jesus is the Resurrection and the Life and the True Light of the world!

"For with You is the fountain of life; in Your light do we see light." Psalm 36:9

CREDIT: I want to give credit to my son Richard. When he was in high school, he explained to his friend the triune nature of God with one sentence! He used the illustration of light being both wave and particle. I was amazed! His friend instantly seemed to understand this explanation!

THE SPIRIT OF THE LORD

And so in that Light, we now encounter the Holy Spirit. There's a sweet **JOY** in His Presence. If you don't know what it's like, you're missing out. The Spirit of the LORD comes in and it is evident! In a corporate meeting, the LORD will make His Presence known, unless the church has had "Ichabod" written on it: "The glory has departed from Israel" 1 Samuel 4:21 Sadly, that is true for many churches in America. The glory has departed them! Seek out a church where the Presence enters.

You can feel the excitement in a church. People want to be there! The glory of the LORD is here amongst the people. The Presence may particularly move on a rhythm of worship or it may be in prayer or it may be in a prophetic word.

We were at a concert inside a grand old church. Mostly everyone there was a music minister or in the choir. The whole cathedral filled with praising and singing, right to the rafters! It was glorious!

We were starting a new church. We all prayed that the Spirit would be evident. I actually prayed for it to be "like electricity." It was! The Spirit came in and it *was* "like electricity."

The joy comes in and His Presence is felt in the spirit of unity. I have often stood back and watched as the Father was pleased with this unity, this unity of the fellowship of Christ.

Sometimes it is often a solemn time. No one says a word for the Holy Presence is perceived. It is still.

"Be still, and know that I am God. I will be exalted among the nations, I will be exalted in the earth!" Psalm 46:10

The LORD is omniscient and everywhere. This is true. But there is a special Presence of the LORD. He can come when hearts are ready to receive Him. That is immeasurable JOY.

ON EARTH AS IT IS IN HEAVEN

"Splendor and majesty are before Him;
strength and JOY are in His place."
1 Chronicles 16:27

The LORD will someday dwell in the New Jerusalem.

"And I heard a loud voice from the throne saying, 'Behold, the dwelling place of God is with man. He will dwell with them, and they will be His people, and God Himself will be with them as their God.'" Revelation 21:3

Yes, God will dwell here, the new heaven and the new earth!

"But will God indeed dwell on the earth? Behold, heaven and the highest heaven cannot contain You ..." 1 Kings 8:27

"Let the heavens be glad, and let the earth **rejoice**; let the sea, and all that fills it; let the field exult, and everything in it! Then shall all the trees of the forest **sing for joy** before the LORD, for He comes, for He comes to judge the earth. Psalm 96:11-13a

God is seated on the throne of heaven and He's moving it here! We await!

"Your kingdom come, your will be done, on earth as it is in heaven." Matthew 6:10

God's will *will* be done. His ideal is for the new heaven and new earth under the reign of the LORD Jesus Christ. It is not of death, but of life!

"Earnest expectation, Of the new creation, Awaits the revelation Of the Sons of God. Clothed in His righteousness, Prepared in holiness." (*Arise!* my words, based on Romans 8:19-21)

This is the grand finale of human history: when human beings are transfigured, led by the Spirit of God, and rule and reign with the LORD Jesus Christ as its head.

"Yet you have made him a little lower than the heavenly beings and crowned him with glory and honor." Psalm 8:5

God's intention, according to the Word of God, is for Jesus Christ to lovingly save many and bring **"many sons to glory"**! So the LORD "is not ashamed to call them brothers." Hebrews 2:10-11

The zenith comes when the LORD will marry His Bride. "Let us **rejoice** and **exult** and give Him the glory, for the marriage of the Lamb has come, and His Bride has made herself ready" Revelation 19:7

The LORD is faithful and true. The King has a covenant marriage and will never, never divorce His wife. They will be one forever.

"You shall no more be termed Forsaken, and your land shall no more be termed Desolate, but you shall be called My Delight Is in Her, and your land Married; for the LORD delights in you, and your land shall be married." Isaiah 62:4

The LORD Jesus Christ will *be* with His Bride by His side. Oh, I can't think of anything more lovely, more superb, more glorious! And we will see His face as if we had been hidden from His reality for so long. In the fullness of time, we shall see His face.

"They [the saints of God] will see His face, and His name will be on their foreheads. And night will be no more. They will need no light of lamp or sun, for the Lord God will be their light, and they will reign forever and ever." Revelation 22:4-5

Oh, yes! And that will be sheer **JOY** and bliss!

"The Spirit and the Bride say, 'Come.'"
Revelation 22:17

He is my **JOY OF JOYS!**

Seal Me Upon Your Heart

Your Presence, O Lord, is sweet, oh so sweet
Let me draw near to You, let me sit at Your feet.
My heart yearns for You, my heart leaps to sing!
Take me, dear Lord, safely under Your wing.

I yearn for You!
I yearn for You!
Seal me upon Your heart.
Seal me upon Your heart.

Your banner, O King, is set over me
Let the nations know, let the whole world see:
My Beloved is mine, and I am Yours
Embrace me, Jesus, evermore.

I am my Beloved's. His desire's towards me.
Make haste, my sweet King, come quickly to me.
The Spirit and the Bride, they say,
"Come, Lord, come.
Come quickly, Jesus, come, oh come."

© 1993 HIM/CAVenable

RESURRECTION GLORY

"They quickly left the tomb and ran, still terrified, but full of unspeakable joy, to carry the news to His disciples." Matthew 28:8 (Weymouth New Testament)

We, who believe in Jesus Christ of Nazareth, have the victory over death itself! The meaning of "death" is actually "separation." It's a separation from the LIFE of God.

Just as a leaf separated from a tree will lose it's life, turning brown and brittle over time, when we separate ourselves from God who is LIFE, we immediately start to die. But calling on the mighty name of Jesus reconnects us to the Tree of Life! He pulls us back to Him when we call on His name!

"And it shall come to pass that everyone who calls upon the name of the Lord shall be saved.'" Acts 2:21 (Quoting Joel 2:32)

In calling on the name of Jesus, "I AM salvation," we call upon LIFE itself!

What is remarkable is that there is SO MUCH LIFE in Christ that when He Himself resurrected from the dead, so did all the saints buried in Jerusalem!

"The tombs also were opened. And many bodies of the saints who had fallen asleep [died physically] were raised, and coming out of the tombs after His resurrection they went into the holy city and appeared to many." Matthew 27:52-53

Now that is amazing! Hundreds of dead people were brought back to LIFE! Christ restored new life!

Our physical bodies may die one day, and that is necessary because they are not suitable at all for LIFE in heaven. We will have spiritual bodies.

"So is it with the resurrection of the dead. What is sown is perishable; what is raised is imperishable. It is sown in dishonor; it is raised in glory. It is sown in weakness; it is raised in power. It is sown a natural body; it is raised a spiritual body." 1 Corinthians 15:42-44

Wow! A spiritual body! Someday, when Jesus returns, we will all receive a new resurrected body just like our Savior. After all, we can't live in heaven without bodies made for heaven! A deep-sea diver cannot deep-sea dive without a special deep-sea diving suit. An astronaut must wear a space suit. Our current bodies are bodies God designed for this earth. Our resurrected spiritual bodies are God's design for heaven, our true home. And so shall we ever live with the LORD in bliss! That is sublime JOY!

"For I am sure that neither death, nor life, nor angels nor rulers, nor things present, nor things to come, nor powers, nor height nor depth, nor anything else in all creation, will be able to separate us from the love of God in Christ Jesus our Lord." Romans 8:38-39

The problem of sin was dealt with and nothing shall separate us from the love of God! The tremendous facts are this:

"that Christ died for our sins in accordance with the Scriptures, that He was buried, that He was raised on the third day in accordance with the Scriptures." 1 Corinthians 15:3b-4

This is the reason for our joy! Christ is raised! But we are to be raised, too!

"But in fact, Christ has been raised from the dead, the firstfruits of those who have fallen asleep. For as by a man came death, by a man has come also the resurrection of the dead. For as in Adam all die, so also in Christ shall all be made alive." 1 Corinthians 15:20-22

The joy of being alive in Christ! We are already alive, those who have faith in Christ, but it's still a time of blossoming! On the third day, we will arise, according to the Scriptures. We have the seed of LIFE.

"After two days He will revive us; on the third day He will raise us up, that we may live before Him." Hosea 6:2

Jesus proclaimed, "I AM the Resurrection and the Life. Whoever believes in Me, though he die, yet shall he live and everyone who lives and believes in Me, shall never die. Do you believe this?" John 11:25

That's a weighty question: "Do you believe this?"

Believing in Jesus reopens the pathway for His LIFE to flow back into us!

Jesus is God. He gives life and He is Life. That's why Jesus came back to life after they crucified Him. Life is more powerful than death! Life just *is*. God *is*. That is the meaning of His name, YHWH, the Great I AM, "who was and is and is to come!" Revelation 4:8

So we await the day when Jesus Christ will put an end to death.

"Then Death and Hades were thrown into the lake of fire." Revelation 20:14

"The last enemy to be destroyed is death." 1 Corinthians 15:26

"When the perishable puts on the imperishable, and the mortal puts on immortality, then shall come to pass the saying that is written:

"Death is swallowed up in victory."

"O death, where is your victory?

O death, where is your sting?"

The sting of death is sin, and the power of sin is the law. But thanks be to God, who gives us the victory through our Lord Jesus Christ." 1 Corinthians 15:54-57

Oh, we have victory in Jesus because Jesus is LIFE. Death will be no more in our existence! Glory to God! LIFE conquers all!

A documentary expressed how life re-instated itself after the disaster of the Chernobyl meltdown. The flora would just grow, and grow, and grow. It took over the abandoned buildings. Plants sprang to life in whatever way it could. If this is an example of natural life, how much more could be the spiritual life? Oh, what we have to look forward to!

We have faith in Christ Jesus, the First-fruits of LIFE. On the third day, He will raise us up! And that's truly a **JOY UNSPEAKABLE!**

IN CONCLUSION

I said it before: sometimes I feel like a wimp. I say "feel" because in the spirit I am a prayer warrior. I read a prayer chain letter on Sri Lanka. It had an article about Christians having "missing limbs." Here, I was crying over my fractured right arm!

Physically, it wasn't a good year for me: a stroke and then, on top of that, my broken arm. But that's my flesh. The joy of the Lord will be my strength. I sing that. I know that. I must get into my spirit-man. That's where there is **JOY!**

I wondered earlier about not hearing from the LORD when I was ill. I know the answer. The Holy Spirit was strong! I was speaking in tongues and the Holy Spirit was moving <u>through me</u>. That was the Holy Spirit! We seem to neglect this part of the triune God, this part that we believers all have! The Holy Spirit *is* the Holy Spirit of Christ and Christ is God! (Romans 8:91; Peter 1:11)

Being sick, it was an excellent time to reflect, to distill, and to write this book. I am so ever grateful. The writing of this book has given me great **JOY!** It has caused me to bring to remembrance the graciousness of the LORD and His glorious salvation. It has reminded me of my predestination as a Bride of Christ, a destiny - with others of like-mindedness - like no other! Oh, how I love Him!

"My beloved speaks and says to me:
'Arise, my love, my beautiful one, and come away!'"

Song of Solomon 2:10

To the ones who will explore with Christ the richness of His Majesty:

"But, as it is written, 'What no eye has seen, nor ear heard, nor the heart of man imagined, what God has prepared for those who love Him'"

1 Corinthians 2:9

Glory be! Oh, I **exceedingly rejoice with joy, joy, JOY!**

PS: I finished writing this book and I "leaped for joy" in my spirit, singing "Glory, Glory, Hallelujah!"